MOW

THE
GRAND
ESSENTIALS

THE GRAND ESSENTIALS

BEN PATTERSON

WORD BOOKS
PUBLISHER
WACO, TEXAS

A DIVISION OF
WORD, INCORPORATED

THE GRAND ESSENTIALS
Copyright © 1987 by Word, Incorporated

Unless otherwise indicated, all Scriptural quotations are from the New International Version of the Bible, published by the Zondervan Corporation, copyright © 1973 by the New York Bible Society, used by permission.

The quotation from "The Part You Wrote for Me," words and music by Sheldon Curry, is copyright © 1977 by Word Music (A Division of Word, Inc.). All rights reserved. International copyright secured. Used by permission. As recorded by Joni Eareckson Tada on JONI'S SONG, Word Records.

Library of Congress Cataloging in Publication Data

Patterson, Ben, 1942–
    The grand essentials.

    1. Work (Theology)   2. God—Worship and love.
3. Public worship.   4. Hope—Religious aspects—
Christianity.   I. Title.
BT738.5.P33   1988   233   87–23142
ISBN 0–8499–0532–X

Printed in the United States of America
7898 RRD 987654321

Contents

Foreword

No more fitting person could have written this book on the seeming paradox of work and worship than our friend, Ben Patterson, himself a man of intriguing contradictions.

The first evening the two of us heard Ben Patterson preach at a Bible Conference, David was so stirred, he felt impelled to walk late into the night to grapple with the deep emotions that were awakened within. This is no easy task, moving the professional communicator who brings a critical ear and hard-won evaluation skills to the verbal efforts of his ministering peers. All too often he or she finds many of them lacking.

But Ben, physically rugged, brings original intellectuality to his platform delivery. He looks like an outdoorsman, or a motorcyclist, one of the guys; then he surprises us by bringing lucid, qualitative content to his sermon. One is compelled to walk, to interact with what has been heard, to grapple with the rationalities that seem to bump, then synthesize, then cohere.

This book is typically Ben. It delivers truths in a way that forces the reader to review previous prejudices about work as well as inadequate past experiences regarding worship. For, truthfully, the average Christian doesn't know how to find meaning in work *or* worship. Consequently, he or she attempts to find meaning apart from both. We need to learn to work in a truly Christian way; we need to learn to worship in a truly Christian way.

Ben understands that "Worship is the liturgy of the sanctuary. Work is the liturgy of the world." What's more he helps his reader comprehend how these two seemingly contradictory activities can become complementary.

Consequently, we recommend:

- That you take this book about work along on a vacation;
- or that you read about worship while riding the commuter train on your way to another eight hours at the job;
- or that you give a copy to your pastor and ask him to preach a series of sermons on the topic of weekday work;
- or that you discuss the meaning of worship at coffee break with co-workers who attend church anywhere;
- or that you read about work and discuss your observations in an elective Sunday school class;
- or that you relax with this book with the impressive title of *The Grand Essentials* sometime when you have a few hours with nothing better to do!

Then let the paradoxes bump, strike deep chords within, cohere and be glad that the Lord prompted a man like Ben Patterson to tackle this topic.

DAVID AND KAREN MAINS
The Chapel of the Air, Inc.

PART I

Something to Do

An unfulfilled vocation drains the
color from a man's entire existence.

Balzac

PROLOGUE I: ∿

Something to Do

Rules for happiness? When I first saw them I was suspicious. *Rules* for happiness? But I couldn't forget them. Later I discovered that what I read was a slight corruption of a statement made by the Scottish cleric and philosopher, Thomas Chalmers. His original was better; he called them "grand essentials":

The grand essentials for happiness are:

> something to do,
> something to love and
> something to hope for.

Borrring!

The more I think about these, the more sense they make to me. Take the first grand essential: *something to do.* I am the father of four small children. The most irritatingly chronic complaint they bring to me is, "Daddy, I'm bored," pronounced, "borrrred." Trying unsuccessfully to suppress

13

the anger in my voice, I ask, "What do you mean, you're bored?" Arms hanging listlessly at their sides, they explain to me that they have nothing to do, pronounced, "doooo." I counter that there are all kinds of things to do, and proceed to tick them off, one by one. If you are a parent, you already know what my children will say to each of my suggestions: "But that's boring too."

What they mean is this: they want to do something that matters to them. It seems the things that matter greatly to me do not always matter greatly to them. Their desire to do something that matters is a universal human trait. We all want to have something to do that matters, really matters. Don't we?

High Level Work

God has given us something to do that really matters. His first command to the first man and woman was to do a great work. He said, "Be fruitful and increase in number; fill the earth and subdue it. Rule over the fish of the sea and the birds of the air and over every living creature that moves on the ground" (Gen. 1:28).

Now that is something to do—to fill the earth and rule it and care for it under God! This is the kind of work that can bring happiness to anyone who will do it! To be given the command to rule the earth and care for it is to be given nothing less than the gift of dignity and meaning—of doing something on earth like the very thing that God himself does.

We all have work to do, high level work: the management of God's creation. This is the vocation of every man, woman, boy and girl on the face of the earth. All our jobs, all the things we do to make a living and secure our daily bread, however small—driving a bus, painting signs, answering the telephone, programming computers—can be seen in the light of this command to manage the earth. When we discover that truth for ourselves, we discover both who we are and what is our true happiness. Then the color comes back into our existence.

> God even milks the cow through you.
>
> *Martin Luther*

1 ∾

Work—Blessing or Curse?

"Hi-ho, hi-ho, it's off to work we go!" If you saw Walt Disney's classic movie, "Snow White and the Seven Dwarfs," you will remember those lines from the song the dwarfs sang as they marched off to work. There was a purposeful joy in their faces and voices as they sang and carried their shovels and pickaxes into the mines.

I saw a variation of that song and its words on a bumper sticker. It said, "I owe, I owe, it's off to work I go." The change is not subtle, it's radical. In so much of life today drudgery has replaced joy, and brute necessity has replaced purpose.

Why Do You Work?

Perhaps the Disney characters could sing the way they did because the film was made on the heels of the Great Depression when so many were out of work. With the economy on the upswing, people were thrilled to be able to work—at anything. That was my father's era, and to his dying day he never stopped being grateful, proud and relieved that he was able to put in a day's work, to feed and clothe his family without any government hand-outs. To him, work meant dignity and manhood.

Perhaps the sentiment of that bumper sticker is a reflection of a generation that works for altogether different reasons. At the very least, it seems to say that work is something we must do whether or not we want to. Or that work is the thing we must do if we are to acquire all the consumer goods we want—and the penalty we must pay when we have acquired too much too soon.

Why do you work? For you is it, "Hi-ho, hi-ho!"? Or is it, "I owe, I owe!"? Is work a blessing or a curse?

Essential to Our Humanness

The Bible's unequivocal answer to this question is that work was created by God as a blessing, a gift. Before God commanded us to work, he blessed us. Then, immediately afterward, he issued his work command. In Genesis 1:28, it was first, "God blessed them . . ." then, "and said to them, 'Be fruitful and increase in number; fill the earth and subdue it. Rule over the fish of the sea and the birds of the air and over every living creature that moves on the ground.'" When God placed the first man in the Garden of Eden, he intended for Adam to "work it and take care of it" (Gen. 2:15). Work had a place—a central place—even in paradise.

A common misconception has the Bible teaching that work is God's curse, or punishment for sin. But the command to work was given as a gift and a blessing before the fall, before sin and punishment entered the picture, not after.

Work is a gift and a blessing from God. And much more, to work is to do something essential to our humanness. The Bible goes so far as to make the startling assertion that to work is to do a godlike thing. Christians have long puzzled over just what it was God meant when he said, "Let us make man in our image, in our likeness" (Gen. 1:26a). The place to start in understanding what he meant is in the very next phrase: "and let them rule over the fish of the sea and the birds . . . , livestock, . . . and over all the creatures that move along the ground" (Gen. 1:26b).

Those two phrases—"Let us make man in our image," and "Let them rule"—must be taken together. Each modifies the other. To be like God is to rule the earth as he does. To rule the earth as he does is to be like God. Throughout the first chapter of Genesis God himself is seen to be a worker, making the heavens, earth, mountains, lakes, forests and all that lives and breathes. When he comes to the creation of man and woman, he makes us workers, too—like himself! It must have been this passage that moved the Reformer Ulrich Zwingli (1484–1531) to say, "There is nothing in the universe so like God as the worker."

Stewards of the Creation

The word that best describes our relationship to God and his creation is steward. It's a somewhat archaic word, but it's valuable because we have no modern word that expresses exactly what it means. A steward is someone entrusted with another's wealth or property and charged with the responsibility of managing it in the owner's best interests.

What a piece of property we have been given to manage: God's creation! A few years ago the Albertson's supermarket chain ran a series of ads that emphasized the personal investment and pride each of its employees had in the quality of its stores. The one I remember best showed an Italian man standing surrounded by tables of fresh vegetables. He was singing, "It's Joe Albertson's supermarket, but the produce department is mine." He saw himself as a steward. He was handed a piece of Joe Albertson's supermarket and given the dignity of managing it as though he were Mr. Joe Albertson himself.

That is the relationship each of us has toward God and his creation. God has given each of us a particular set of talents and gifts. He has given each of us a piece of time and space. All that we are and own come from him, and he has charged us with the responsibility of managing these things as though we were God himself! Let the artist do art to the glory of God. Let the banker bank to the glory of God. Let the farmer farm to the glory of God. Let the time you have be managed to the glory of God. Let your personality show his goodness.

True Dignity

Our dignity as humans comes not from what we have— for everything we have belongs to God. Psalm 24:1: "The earth is the Lord's and everything in it." That "everything" includes our time, our wealth, our abilities, our careers— everything. We're inclined to think that what we have is our own and any excess belongs to God. Our attitude toward stewardship is something like the alleged new "short form" from the Internal Revenue Service that was circulating around my town last year. It had only four questions:

(1) What was your income last year?
(2) What were your expenses?
(3) How much do you have left?
(4) Send it in.

If God took from us what was his, he would collect before expenses, not after! Paul told Timothy, "We brought nothing into the world, and we can take nothing out of it" (1 Tim. 6:17). We entered paupers, we will exit paupers.

Our dignity comes not from what we have, for everything we have comes from God. Our dignity comes from what we have done with what has been given to us. It comes from answering God's call to be stewards of his creation.

The most poignant instance of this dignity I have ever heard comes from a story Gordon Cosby tells of his first pastorate in a little Baptist church in the deep South. In his congregation, there was a widow woman with six children. She was supporting her family on a paltry wage of $40.00 a month. One day, while going through the church records, Cosby was astonished to discover that this woman was giving the church $4.00 a month—a tithe of her meager income! He brought this to the attention of the deacons who, as he was, were astonished and embarrassed that the church was taking money from this poor woman. Why, the church should be giving her money, not the other way around!

The deacon board instructed Cosby to make a pastoral call and let her off the hook. He visited the lady and told her she need not feel any obligation to give to the church, but should keep the money for herself and her children. He writes, "I am not wise now, I was less wise then. I went and told her of the concern of the deacons. I told her as graciously and as supportively as I knew how that she was relieved of the responsibility of giving. As I talked with her . . . tears came to her eyes. 'I want to tell you,' she said, 'that you are taking away the last thing that gives my life dignity and meaning.'"[1]

That lady knew what it meant to be a human being, made in the image of God. Her dignity as a person was grounded not in what she had, but in what she did with what she had! She had the honor of being a steward of the little section of the world God had given her in trust.

Work and Marriage

Even something as essential to our humanness as marriage finds part of its meaning in the light of God's call to work as his stewards. When God placed Adam in the Garden of Eden to work it and take care of it, he decided that it wasn't good for man to be alone there. He needed a helper. The animals were considered as possibilities, but soon rejected, because, in the words of Scripture, "no suitable helper was found." So what did God do? He created Eve. God's response to Adam's need for a helper in his work was to create Eve—and the institution of marriage.

There are two images of marriage in the Bible. One is very popular today, the other has all but been ignored. The first is of two people gazing into each other's eyes. It speaks of intimacy and deep personal encounter and dominates the modern imagination. Its fullest expression in the Bible is in the lovely Song of Solomon.

There is a second image, equally biblical, and much in need today to balance the first. It is of two people gazing, not at each other, but in the same direction, shouldering the same burden. It speaks of work to do together that simply cannot be done well alone. Its fullest expression is found in the second chapter of Genesis.

Without this second image of marriage guiding us, marriages become narcissistic and self-absorbed; and they often collapse under the weight of expectations heaped upon them. With it, our marriages can have the balance of both the inward and the outward perspective. When couples realize that there is more to a marriage than personal fulfillment— that they have a work to do together for the glory of God—a fresh wind blows into their relationship. Happily, personal fulfillment is then given as a by-product of a larger activity; not the ever-elusive pot of gold to be sought at the end of the rainbow. As David says,

> . . . the work of your fingers,
> the moon and the stars,
>   which you have set in place,
> what is man that you are mindful of him,
>   the son of man that you care for him? . . .
>   and crowned him with glory and honor (Ps. 8:3–5).

What indeed is man? What could he be in all of that? Yet, wonder of wonders:

> You made him a little lower than the heavenly beings
>   and crowned him with glory and honor.
> You made him ruler over the works of your hands;
>   you put everything under his feet . . . .

O Lord, our Lord,
　how majestic is your name in all the earth! (Ps. 8:5, 9).

Apparently, part of the majesty of God's name in all the earth is the work of his humanity, made like him, ruling as he would.

What a mystery our humanness is! God completes his creative work, then stands back from it and stoops to let us be his partners, or collaborators. A prosperous farmer invited his pastor over for dinner after church one Sunday. After the customary fried chicken and apple pie, the farmer took the parson on a walk around his farm. They hiked to the top of a hill near the house to get a panorama of the place. All around them, for acres and acres, there were beautifully kept orchards, straight rows of crops, geometric patches in varying shades of green. The pastor began to rhapsodize: "O look! God is so wonderful! How beautiful are the works of his hands." The farmer looked at his guest quizzically and replied, "I'm sure you are right, pastor. But you should have seen this place when God had it all to himself, before I got my hands on it."

God supplies us with the creation and charges us to cultivate it. He gives us nature and bids us create culture. His are the raw materials, ours is the craftsmanship. But none of this is ours independent of God, apart from him. The creation is ours under God, in dependence on him. Martin Luther was right when he said, "God even milks the cow through you."

What a mystery this is! In our work we can actually do something like the thing God did in his work of creation. Our work is usually so familiar and routine that we never stand back to really see and be awed by the wonder of the brute fact that we can work. A little girl was drawing a picture as her proud father watched over her shoulder. Beaming, he said to her, "That's so good, honey. How is it you can draw so well?" The girl furrowed her brow and thought for a moment, as only children will think, about that kind of question. Then she answered, "First I think. And then I draw my think."

That is what work is: drawing our think! There is the world out there. There is something lacking in it, something that needs to be done: the dishes washed, the oil changed, the checkbook balanced, the baby's diaper changed, the atom split, the space shuttle launched. We can think of it and we can apply our hands and our tools to the task and . . . do it!

All work, from the simplest chore to the most challenging and complex undertaking, is a wonder and a miracle. It is a gift and a blessing that God has given us to be something like he is, and to do something like he does: to rule the earth as his stewards. To work is to do something that is essential to our humanness.

Live to Work or Work to Live?

In short, we were created to work. "Work is not, primarily, a thing one does to live," writes Dorothy Sayers, "but the thing one lives to do."[2] It is true that, in most cases, we will not live if we do not work—but this is not the primary reason God made us workers. He made us workers so that we might be like him and have the joy and fulfillment of doing with the world something like the thing he himself does. We were made to work.

Sayers went on to say that if we truly understood what this doctrine of work meant and took it to heart, the results would be revolutionary in our individual lives and in our society. I suspect that the mere mention of them here may cause some anger and befuddlement in many of you who read this. But her conclusions seem to me to be as inescapable as they are trenchant.

Salaries and Profits

Take salaries and profits, for instance. If we truly believed and ordered our lives according to the biblical idea of work we would be asking a brand new set of questions about them. We would ask of a person not, "How much does she make?" but "What is her work worth?" And we wouldn't ask of our work, "How much will this work pay?" but "Is it good work?"

The Bible knows nothing of a hierarchy of labor. No work is degrading. If it ought to be done, then it is good work. King Saul could plow his field with his oxen and not detract one whit from his dignity as king of Israel. Indeed, there are some kinds of work in which the pay is extremely high and the work's value is extremely low, seen in the light of our call to be stewards of God's creation.

The great Japanese Christian Kagawa was to be honored one time at a banquet. On the way to the banquet hall, he and his entourage stopped in a restroom. The men entered the banquet hall. They had all sat down at their table before anyone noticed that the guest of honor was missing. They looked everywhere until someone thought to check back in the restroom. There was Kagawa, picking up the paper towels someone had left on the floor! No work is beneath the dignity of a man or woman who understands that dignity comes from being a steward, not doing a particular kind of work.

If we truly ordered our lives according to the biblical idea of work, we would ask of ourselves and our work, not "How much will I make?" but "Will this work use my abilities and gifts to the fullest?" Manufacturers and advertisers would stop asking, "How can we get people to buy this thing?" and ask instead, "Is this thing worth buying?"

Sayers writes: "We have all got it fixed in our heads that the proper end of work is to be paid for—to produce a return in profits or payment to the worker which fully or more compensates the effort he puts into it."[3] But that is not the proper end of work. The proper end of work is to give glory to God by obeying his command to rule the earth as his partners and stewards.

If we cannot see the work we do as in some way the fulfillment of our call to be like God and to exercise his love and authority over the creation, then one of two things is wrong. Either we lack the vision or skill to see, and should ask God for clarity to relate the work we do to his purposes; or the work we are doing is unworthy and we should promptly get out of it.

It's not that the desire for a salary or profit is wrong. It is just that, at best, it is a secondary question, and at worst a destructive one. A salary and a profit should be the by-product of good work well done; not the reason for the work in the first place. When they become the chief reason for our work, then our work ceases to be for the glory of God and becomes something we do for our own glory. When that happens, our work goes sour.

Work and Leisure

If we truly believed and ordered our lives according to the biblical idea of work, we would also take on a new attitude toward both work and leisure. If we really believed that work is something for which God made us—that we live to work, not work to live—then we would not look upon our work as something we must hurry up to get done so we can get on with our play. We would look upon our play and rest as a change of pace or rhythm that refreshed us for the delightful purpose of getting back to the work God created us to do.

Charles Schulz, the creator of the popular cartoon strip, "Peanuts," was interviewed in the *Los Angeles Times*. He talked about the amazement of guests who come to his home and learn about how far ahead he has to work. He said,

> A visitor almost never fails to remark: "Gee, you could work real hard, couldn't you, and get several months ahead and then take the time off?"
> Being . . . a slow learner, it took me until last year to realize what an odd statement that really is. You don't work all of your life to do something so you don't have to do it. I could talk about Beethoven knocking out a few fast symphonies so he could take some time off; or Picasso grinding

out a dozen paintings so he could go away, but the comparison would obviously be pompous.
    We live in a society that worships vacations.[4]

I would add, we also live in a society that worships retirement. How odd that we should spend all our lives doing
something so we don't have to do it anymore. That is not to
say that we should not retire, but we should be cautious about
retirement. We should look critically at the notion that the
good life is to be rewarded for long years of labor with an
extended season of recreation and play in our twilight years.
We should see retirement instead as perhaps a time to slow
down, but not stop what we are doing—if health permits; or
perhaps a time to embark on a brand new field of endeavor
altogether!
    I love what my mother- and father-in-law are doing in
their retirement. Everything they did before they are doing
now. The only change is that they are now doing these things
at their own pace and in proportions they desire.
    When he wants to, Oliver still teaches music, as he did
for years at Bethel College in St. Paul, Minnesota. In their
younger days, he and his wife Shirley raised six children on a
teacher's salary. They are still at it! Now that the kids are
spread out all over the world, they perform marvelously as
circuit-riding parents to their children and grandchildren.
As I write this they are visiting son Dan and his family in
Zaire, Africa, where Dan is serving for 2½ years as a mis-
sionary. Oliver and Shirley are there helping out with the
kids and doing whatever else needs to be done. Last summer,
when I took my sabbatical, they graciously put my family and
me up for nearly three months so I could get away and research this book. When they are home they are still valued
workers in their church.
    The point is, they are having a lot of fun doing every-
thing they always did before retirement. The only difference
is that now they don't have to get up and go to work every
day. There is a lot less necessity and a lot more freedom in

what they do. Now they do all they did before because they want to be of service. I doubt that they have theologized as much about all this as I have. But they understand, on a deep level, that it is good to work. Work is a blessing, not a curse.

Better Things to Do!

We have better things to do than to stop working! We have work to do that far outshines anything mere play can offer. One day the great artist Leonardo Da Vinci was at work on a canvas he had been toiling over for weeks. The painting was nearly finished and it looked magnificent. The subject had been carefully chosen and it had Leonardo's unique perspective and distinctive choice of colors. Suddenly he stopped, called a student over, handed him the paint brush and said, "Here, you finish it." The student protested that he was not worthy or able to complete so beautiful a painting.

Said Da Vinci, "Will not what I have done inspire you to do your best?"

Will not the masterful work that God has done with his creation inspire us to do our best as his co-workers?

Here lies the body of Thomas Jones,
born a man, died a grocer.

Epitaph, somewhere in Scotland

2 ～

Take This Job and Shove It!

"Take this job and shove it." You can hear those words all the time at the Log Inn—a tavern and restaurant whose clientele is a mixture of white and blue collar workers from nearby offices, warehouses and light industries. Sometimes at lunch I crowd into this smoke-filled dive with them, eat a polish sausage sandwich or a chili dog, and watch and listen as they drink their favorite beverages, shoot a little pool, bet on the next football game and shout as they try to hear one another over the blare of the jukebox.

Ah, the jukebox. What it plays is as much a commentary on the lives of those who put their quarters into it as the cars they drive, the clothes they wear and the brand of beer they drink. Judging from the amount of playing time, the number one song is a country and western number by Johnny Paycheck, "Take This Job and Shove It!"

Apparently most Americans would like to tell their bosses and corporations to take their jobs and shove them. After scores of interviews with men and women from a wide variety of workplaces, author Studs Terkel concluded in his bestseller, *Working:* "This book, being about work, is, by its very nature, about violence—to the spirit as well as to the body. It is about ulcers as well as accidents, about shouting matches as well as fistfights, about nervous breakdowns as well as kicking the dog around. It is, above all (or beneath all), about daily humiliations. To survive the day is triumph enough for the walking wounded among the great many of us."[1]

The Money, the Boss and the System

Clearly something has gone wrong with work. God made us to be workers, not "walking wounded." From the beginning he gave us work as a gift and a blessing, an essential ingredient of our humanness. It was his original intent that we live to work, not work to live. But for many the opposite is true; work is something they do to live, period—if you can call it living. What went wrong with work?

There are all kinds of answers to that question. Most of those I hear have something to do with the money, the boss or the system; things like low salaries, poor working conditions, jackass supervisors or boring and meaningless tasks.

The Bible has but one answer to the question, "What went wrong with work?" *Sin.* It's not that any of these other answers is wrong. There is truth in them all. But sin is the root and they are just some of the branches of the tree. Sin is the disease and the money, the boss and the system are but some of its symptoms.

What is sin and how has it affected our work? Go back for a moment to the first two chapters of the Book of Genesis, where God gives the first man and woman, Adam and Eve, the command to work. He commands them to rule over the earth and care for it as his stewards. A steward is someone entrusted with another person's property and given the responsibility of managing it in the owner's interests.

Two Extraordinary Trees—God's Great Risk

The first job God gives these two stewards is a garden to care for. Among the things growing there are two very extraordinary trees standing side by side in the center of the garden: the tree of life and the tree of the knowledge of good and evil. As Adam and Eve do their gardening God tells them they may eat of the tree of life. That tree is an image of the life and fulfillment which comes from work done as God created it to be done. In effect, it says the tree Adam and Eve cultivate in the garden, that is, the very work they do there, has in it the possibility of life.

The other tree is something else altogether. It is called the tree of the knowledge of good and evil. Of it, God says to Adam: "You must not eat of the tree of the knowledge of good and evil, for when you eat of it you will surely die" (Gen. 2:17). It presents Adam and Eve with a choice: whether to work in obedience to God or in disobedience to him.

Think of it. Among the things Adam is to care for as a worker-steward are two wonderful and mysterious trees. These two trees tell us that involved in the gift of work are the monumental issues of life and death and good and evil. Man has a choice between these opposites. Mankind is God's great risk, for only he has the freedom to choose, for God or against him. With the godlike gift of work comes a godlike power and possibility, the freedom to say yes or no to our Creator.

The message of the Bible is that Adam and Eve, and every son and daughter of Adam and Eve, have eaten of the fruit God commanded us not to eat. In other words, they and we—all of us together—have used our freedom to say no to God. That, in a word, is what sin is; and that, in a word, is what went wrong with work.

Christians have long called this first and archetypical disobedience of Adam and Eve the "Fall." All creation is affected; nothing is left untouched by this primal break with

God. Most important, a fracture now runs right through the
center of four fundamental human relationships: our relationship to God, to ourselves, to each other, and, critical for
the question we are asking—"What went wrong with
work?"—our relationship to the earth and our work upon it.
God says to Adam:

> Because you listened to your wife and ate from the
> tree about which I commanded you, "You must not eat of it,"
> Cursed is the ground because of you;
>   through painful toil you will eat of it all the days
>   of your life.
> It will produce thorns and thistles for you,
>   and you will eat of the plants of the field.
> By the sweat of your brow
>   you will eat of your food
> until you return to the ground,
>   since from it you were taken;
> for dust you are
>   and to dust you will return (Gen. 3:17–19).

The rest, as they say, is history—in more ways than one.
For the Bible would have us to understand that the first couple's story is also our story. "Fallenness" is a condition, a reality into which we all are born. Modern secular analyses of the
human condition tend to see us and our work as something
"not yet" good, something yet to be improved and perfected.
The Bible takes the opposite tack and sees us and our work as
"no longer" good and in need of salvation.

Fallenness is not only a condition into which we are born,
it is something we have also chosen. We too have sinned, each
of us. Each of us shares his or her responsibility for the fallenness of our work. We too have chosen to go our own way in our
work, and we, along with our work, have fallen.

Thankfully, work still retains some of its original beauty
despite the fall. It still can be a source of great joy and
fulfillment. But even when it is good it is broken. It bears the
marks of sin: struggle, futility, greed and anxiety.

Struggle

The first thing sin did and does to work is to make it a struggle. The ground no longer yields the fruit of our labors willingly. God says, *"Cursed is the ground because of you; through painful toil you will eat of it all the days of your life"* (Gen. 3:17). Since the fall, our sustenance comes only after a lot of blood, sweat, toil and sometimes tears. Before the fall, work was a gift, a "may" from God. After the fall work is a demand, a "must." Before, it was a joyful command: "work and eat." Now, it is a bitter necessity: "no work, no eat."

Wrath is the classic theological word used to describe this state of affairs. Wrath is the Bible's word for God's holy anger at sin. In relation to our work it means the work that was once a part of our fellowship with God now becomes an arena—one of the chief ones—in which we experience his resistance and opposition.

Before the fall work was done in communion with God. Now it must be done in the cold, impersonal environment of the so-called "laws" of nature. Work that was once a gift and a freedom is now a constricting necessity. The hard fact of our existence is this: we all simply must work—and in a world that seems to be indifferent to our needs. Those who are not forced to work are a tiny minority, and often their freedom from work is purchased at the price of the slavery of many others. Even those of us who have some freedom to decide what kind of work we will do are a minority. The only choice the rest of the world has, says Tom Sine, is upon which shoulder to carry the burden. The earth that once yielded its fruit so willingly must now be wrestled for its food.

In the Broadway musical "Porgy and Bess," the black slave says what is true for us all, in one way or another. He toils and strains upon an "old man" river, that just keeps on rolling along, deaf and blind to his misery, mute to yield any of its wisdom.

Futility

With the struggle of work comes also a tragic ironic twist. The very earth that so reluctantly and indifferently feeds Adam will one day swallow him up! Note the way God puts it to Adam: "You will wrestle your food from the ground all the days of your life; until you return to the ground, since from it you were taken; for dust you are and to dust you shall return" (Gen. 3:19). The very sweat and strain we expend to stay alive will one day kill us. Our wrestling with the earth is also a wrestling with death.

We hardly need to read the Bible to know this is true. G. K. Chesterton said that of all Christian doctrines, the doctrine of the fall, or original sin, is the only one that can be empirically proven. We see evidences all around us of the deadening impact of work. For instance, pick up the Sunday classified section of any metropolitan newspaper and read the ads for work trauma hotlines and work injury and stress evaluation centers. Typical are these from the *Los Angeles Times*:

> Job pressures too much? Overworked? Harassed at work? Headaches? Poor Sleep? Stomach aches? Depressed? Nervous/Irritable? Chest pain? Unfairly fired? Mistreated? Call us now for immediate help! You may receive treatment and Money Benefits AT NO COST TO YOU! ALL APPOINTMENTS FREE! Take charge. End your distress now. You are not alone. STOP STRESS NOW. We care!

When we fell our work fell with us, and the fall has cast a deathly pall of futility over our work. Where does it all get us, except to the grave? My dad died of a massive coronary at age 59—prematurely, I believe. A sense of grinding necessity dominated everything he did. When he was working it was to pay the bills. When he wasn't working he was worrying about the bills. As I tried to sort through his personal papers after his death I found several bundles of check stubs and receipts wrapped in rubber bands. I sighed as I looked at these mementos of his struggle with work and death. What did any of them matter now? But God said it would be that way. The earth (upon which we were created to exercise a godlike dominion) had swallowed my dad up in death—as it will swallow you and me.

There is an epitaph on a gravestone somewhere in Scotland that sums this all up pretty neatly. It reads, "Here lies the body of Thomas Jones, born a man, died a grocer." God created work to be something for man and woman to do, and in the doing be something like God himself. Psalm 8 says he made us a little lower than the angels, crowned us with glory and honor and made us rulers over his creation. Instead, the tendency of work in a fallen world is to make the worker not the ruler, but the slave of the work—not a little lower than the angels, but a little less than human.

Greed and Anxiety

When work is shot through with struggle and a sense of futility, it usually causes anxiety as well. The third chapter of Genesis does not address this issue directly, but the theme runs throughout Scripture and is epitomized in Jesus' parable of the Rich Fool. After man enjoys a year of bumper crops, he says to himself, "What am I to do with all this wealth? I know! I'll build more and bigger barns and store it all up. Then I can kick back and relax; take life easy and eat, drink and be merry." Jesus called this man a fool because he spent all his time and energy taking care of himself and getting richer in the process. All the while he was becoming poorer toward God.

Jesus introduced this parable by telling his audience to be on guard against greed of any kind. So it would seem that greed is all he was speaking against in the story. But there was something even more lethal than greed operating in the life of the rich fool. Jesus continues to speak to his disciples after he tells this story and says to them, "Therefore I tell you, *do not worry* about your life, what you will eat; or about your body, what you will wear" (Luke 12:22, italics mine).

Worry, anxiety, insecurity—these are the things that lie behind greed and avarice. In a fallen world, what we receive we get only after a struggle. The pie is only so big and there are far more people who want a piece of it than there are pieces to be had, so it's every man for himself. Someone defined insecurity as discovering on the first day of your new job that your name is written on the door in chalk—and there's a wet sponge hanging next to it! Insecurity is also the feeling in your work that even if you do make your mark in the world there is someone right behind you with an eraser.

But our deepest anxiety, and the source of all others, is that we are cut off, alienated from God because of sin. To be like God, as the serpent promised, is to carry an intolerably heavy burden; it is to be the sole master of our fate. If we don't take care of number one, no one else will.

What we need more than anything else—more than work trauma hotlines and stress reduction centers, more than better bosses, larger pay and better working conditions—is to have healed the broken relationship with God that set all this mess into motion in the first place. Frederick Buechner says "the power of sin is centrifugal." Remove God from the center of a human life or a human society—or a job—and sin will tend to "push everything out toward the periphery. Bits and pieces go flying off the core until only the core is left. Eventually bits and pieces of the core itself go flying off until in the end nothing at all is left. 'The wages of sin is death' is St. Paul's way of saying the same thing."[2]

Unless something can be done to reverse the centrifugal power of sin and reconcile us to God, all our efforts at the reform and renewal of work will eventually come up empty. But can anything be done? Is there anything, or anyone, who can do this? Not from the human side of the problem, says the Bible and, I might add, the sober record of human history.

Nothing short of a miracle will save us and our work. But that is what the Christian gospel claims—the miracle has occurred, the impossible has happened!

Teach me, my God and King,
In all things Thee to see,
And what I do in any thing,
To do it as for Thee.

George Herbert

3 ∼

Is There Any Hope?

Years ago an S–4 submarine was rammed by a ship off the coast of Massachusetts and sank immediately. The entire crew was trapped in a prison house of death. Every effort was made to rescue them but all failed. Near the end of the ordeal, a diver placed his helmeted ear to the side of the vessel and heard a tapping from inside. He recognized it as Morse code. It was a question, forming slowly: "Is . . . there . . . any . . . hope?"

Totally Depraved

Our predicament is like that of the crew in the doomed submarine. God warned Adam and Eve that the sin of rebellion would result in death. As the submarine's collision with the ship, the death that came with their sin was not sudden, but gradual. But sin's symptoms were—and still are—to be seen everywhere: in our relationship to God and in our relationships with each other (and in our relationship to our work). Life has gone on after the fatal catastrophe, but it has been doomed to death ever since. All subsequent living has been lived without hope, under the curse of death.

Sin did not cancel out or completely disfigure the beauty of good work as God intended it to be. It simply placed in it the germ of death and futility. What some theologians call the doctrine of total depravity means just that: every aspect of our lives—even the highest and loveliest—is infected with death. This does not mean that everything human is totally without goodness, that humankind is as bad as it can be. It simply means that everything human is infected with evil—it has the germ of sin and death in it.

The biblical doctrine of total depravity is an outrage to some. Donald Barnhouse told of how Lord Roseberry once looked at his little granddaughter, whom he adored, and exclaimed indignantly, "And the Church calls her a child of wrath!" Yet he would have felt no moral outrage, said Barnhouse, if a doctor had looked at a tiny spot on her arm and said, "This child is a leper." Spiritual death is like physical death; it need be no more than a puncture, an infinitesimal presence, to do its final, deadly work.

"Is . . . there . . . any . . . hope?" That is the question of any man or woman who feels trapped in his or her work. Is there any hope for this struggle and anxiety, for this numbing drudgery and meaninglessness in what I do to make a living? Can there be any life in the work I must do to live?

There is hope, says the gospel of Jesus Christ. Neon signs flashing the message, "Jesus Saves," may be in poor taste, but their theology is impeccable. The apostle Paul writes of Jesus, "For he has rescued us from the dominion of darkness and brought us into the kingdom of the Son he loves, in whom we have redemption, the forgiveness of sins" (Col. 1:13, 14).

Jesus saves! And he saves not just the inner life of our hearts, but also the outer life of our work. The gospel is aimed at our hearts as the center of its attention, but its circumference extends to every dimension of our existence, including our work. In Christ, we and our work are rescued. In Christ, we and our work are redeemed. In Christ, we and the sins we have committed in our work are forgiven.

Reconciliation

How does Jesus save our work from the fatal infection of sin and death? He does it first of all by reconciling us to God. Another word the apostle Paul likes to use for sin and its consequences is "alienated." In the passage just quoted he describes our condition before we met Christ this way: "Once you were alienated from God, and were enemies in your minds because of your evil behavior."

Before Christ the state of affairs between us and God was alienation. "But now," Paul continues, "he has reconciled you by Christ's physical body through death to present you holy in his sight, without blemish and free from accusation. . . ." (Col. 1:21, 22).

By Christ's atoning death on the cross, the reason for the fallenness of our work—our alienation from God because of sin—is healed. The relationship that sin broke is repaired and we are reconciled to God. In some mysterious way, when Christ gave his life *for* the world, he gave his life *to* the world. Faith in that cosmic event reconciles us to God and brings peace into discord, and unity into disunity.

Not Orphans, but Children

When we are reconciled to God, the reason for our struggle with work and all of our restless anxiety in it is removed. For now we are no longer orphans, but children of our Father in heaven. He will take care of us. He will meet our needs.

In the last chapter I said that the rich fool in Jesus' parable is emblematic of men and women without a Father in heaven. Such people must live totally out of their own resources. They are orphans in the world and must do their work and live out their lives in restless anxiety. So in an effort to nail down his security, a man foolishly sets out to build more barns to hold what he has earned. But God calls him a fool because all he has stashed away will mean nothing to him in death.

Jesus finishes his parable and then tells his disciples not to worry about food, clothing and shelter—their security—because they have a Father in heaven to worry about it for them. He says, "Therefore, I tell you, do not worry about your life, what you will eat; or about your body, what you will wear . . . your Father knows that you need them. But seek his kingdom, and these things will be given to you as well" (Luke 12:22, 30b, 31).

That raises an important question. Whose responsibility is it to clothe and feed your family? Do you think it is yours? You're wrong! Jesus says it is God's. You and I have but one responsibility, one thing needful—as obedient children, to do the will of our Father in heaven.

When I was a child it never once occurred to me to worry about whether my mom and dad would be able to pay the rent, buy food or keep our health insurance current. I never lost a moment's sleep over any of these matters. It would have been wrong for me to do so. All I had to concern myself with was simply being a child and obeying my folks. That was my one and only responsibility.

We are children of our Father in heaven! It is improper—an unnatural reversal of roles—for us to feel and act as though we, not God, were the Father. It is worse than improper, it is unconscious blasphemy. For us to worry about our livelihood is to presume to stand in the place that only God should occupy in our lives.

The Miracle of Our Daily Bread

This doesn't mean we don't have to work. It does mean that the work we do is not what is ultimately responsible for our security and well-being. God is. It is he who provides the work and it is he who makes our work fruitful. Jesus never commanded us to work for our daily bread, he commanded us to pray for it. Of the two, work and prayer, it is prayer that is critical. That's because, when it comes to our needs, of the two, us and God, it is God who is critical!

To be reconciled to God, to become a child of your heavenly Father, is to put you and your work in its proper place. I was told an apocryphal story of Bill Russell, the legendary center for the Boston Celtics. If it isn't true, it ought to be. According to the story, he was in the midst of an intense basketball game when, as he ran down court, he burst out laughing. The laughter grew until he had to stop playing and just lean over, his hands on his knees, and guffaw. Coach Red Auerbach called time out and screamed for his seemingly mad center to come over to the sideline. "What on earth are you laughing about?" demanded Auerbach. "You could lose the game for us, you know!"

It took Russell a few moments to regain his composure and explain, "Well, you see, it suddenly hit me—here I am running around in my underwear in front of thousands of people, trying to throw a little ball through a hoop and I'm getting paid to do it!"

The work we do to make a living isn't ridiculous in itself, but it becomes so when we let it make its imperial claims on our lives and tell us that it is the only thing standing between us and poverty, worthlessness or oblivion. God alone is our hope and security.

When God, not the work, is our security, then the work we do can take on a certain joy and even wonder. Sometimes it is the bemusement of a Bill Russell, saying, "I can't believe I get paid to do *this!*" More often it is the amazement of a farmer planting seeds in soil and watching with awe and wonder the miracle of how his daily bread is performed before his very eyes.

We should be careful, however, not to romanticize the farmer's work. Nowadays there is a tendency to see workers like farmers as close to the earth and therefore close to nature—and therefore closer to God. Most of those who think that way have never been farmers, or been around them! The work they do can be just as grinding and boring and frustrating as any other kind of work.

The miracle of the heavenly Father providing food for his children through seeds planted and wheat harvested is no greater or more wonder-full than what happens daily through the work done in our so-called technological world. In his or her own way, the teacher, the waitress, the computer programmer, the mechanic and the corporate executive daily plant seeds that miraculously yield a harvest. The way each of us is fed and clothed is greater than the sum of our economic system's component parts. It is still our Father who feeds and clothes us. The same God who stands sovereign over the laws of nature also holds his kingly scepter over economic systems and the ebb and flow of politics and commerce. And he still cares for his creation and his children.

Immensity Cloistered in a Womb

There is more to what Christ has done to redeem us and our work than reconciling us to God—in a way, something even more basic. He saves our work by his Incarnation.

The supreme mystery of the Christian faith is not the resurrection of Jesus, nor is it his atoning death on the cross, nor the miracles he performed. The supreme mystery of our faith is what C. S. Lewis called the Grand Miracle—the miracle that is the presupposition of all the others, from the feeding of the 5,000 to the empty tomb. It is the startling gospel assertion that in the man Jesus of Nazareth, first century Jew, carpenter and intinerant preacher, God himself, the creator of the universe, took on human flesh!

That is the mystery and miracle of the Incarnation. It says God really took on human flesh, not as in some pagan myths in which the gods might temporarily inhabit a human body, but that he really and truly became fully man and yet remained fully God. He so became one of us that he took the form of an infant in the womb of the Jewish peasant girl, Mary.

Poet John Donne piled paradox upon paradox as he tried to wrap words around this mystery. In his poem, "Annunciation," he said to Mary:

> Ere by the spheres time was created, thou
> Wast in his mind, who is thy Son, and Brother;
> Whom thou conceiv'st, conceiv'd; yea thou art now
> Thy Maker's maker, and thy Father's mother;
> Thou hast light in dark; and shutst in little room
> *Immensity cloistered in thy deare womb.*[1]

Donne is saying, "Think of it, Mary! Before time began you were in the mind of your child. You will be the mother of your Father, the daughter of your Son. You have immensity contained in your womb."

Immensity was cloistered not only in her womb, but in a room—a carpenter shop in Nazareth. There Jesus probably learned and plied the trade of his father Joseph until he began his public ministry. The God who *made* wood, sawed wood and hammered nails, swept the floors, took out the trash and paid the bills!

Clothing the Common with Glory

In the Incarnation, God sanctified the common and made extraordinary the ordinary. This means so much for our mundane labors. William Barclay has written a lovely prayer that captures what this means for our mundane labors:

> O God, our Father, we remember at this time . . . how the eternal Word became flesh and dwelt among us . . . We thank you that Jesus did a day's work like any working-man, that he knew the problem of living together in a family, that he knew the frustration and irritation of serving the public, that he had to earn a living, and to face all the wearing routine of everyday work and life and living, and so *clothed each common task with glory.*[2]

The incarnate Christ broke down once and for all the wall we have erected between the sacred and the secular. He did this in his person, for he was the God-man, the one in whom both the sacred and the secular, the visible and the invisible, lived together in perfect harmony. The Incarnation proclaimed loudly and vigorously what was implicit in what God said when he created the world and pronounced it good—that the material world is a fit vehicle for God to show himself and for us to encounter him.

In 1977 my wife and I toured Israel. There are very few authentic sites in Israel, that is, places we are sure are actually mentioned in the Bible. But one is Gabbatha, or the "pavement," of which John speaks in his Gospel. It is a flat marbled area that was near the judgment seat of Pilate. You can still see there a kind of board game Roman soldiers scratched in the marble. Looking at it, it isn't hard to imagine them loitering there killing time as they waited for Jesus to be brought out before the mob. Perhaps he stood at that very spot. He certainly stood near it.

A church is built right over the site. The place felt holy. We all talked in hushed tones as we looked at that few square feet of ancient marble where the incarnate Son of God had probably stood. But the Incarnation tells us that the Son of God didn't just walk upon the earth, he entered into it in the deepest way conceivable—pun intended! He became a part of it, flesh and blood himself. A church should be built over the whole creation, not just a part of it!

Which is precisely the point. In breaking down the wall between the sacred and the secular, the Incarnation has clothed the common with glory and made it possible for a poet like Gerard Manley Hopkins to write, "The world is charged with the glory of God./It will flame out, like shining from shook foil; . . ."

A Sacramental Presence

The bare fact of the Incarnation rescues us and our work from the dominion of darkness. It does this by making all of life, including our work, an arena in which not only to serve, but to *meet* God. It gives work the possibility of being sacramental. The Anglican Book of Common Prayer defines a sacrament as a visible sign of an invisible reality. In Baptism, water is a sign of the Holy Spirit. In Communion, bread and wine are signs of the body and blood of Christ. The ordinary and common point to the extraordinary and uncommon. The natural mediates the supernatural.

Because of the incarnation, all creation, including work, can be sacramental, in the broadest sense of the word. This is not to say that nine to five is the same as the bread and wine. But the difference between the two is in degree, not in kind. Both the workbench and the Lord's Table can be approached in faith, and when they are, they become visible signs of an invisible reality. For this reason the apostle Paul instructed workers, even slaves, to do their work in faith, "as unto the Lord" himself (Eph. 6:7; Col. 3:23).

Because of the Incarnation, the medieval monk, Brother Lawrence, could fellowship with Christ as he washed the pots and pans in the abbey kitchen. He said he felt no closer to Christ on his knees in prayer or at the altar, than he did at the sink with his hands and arms deep in dishwater. Work had a sacramental quality for Brother Lawrence. For this simple monk, the Incarnation had erased the artificial distinction between the sacred and the secular.

The Elixir for Work

No one understood better the sacramental character of work than the great seventeenth century poet and priest George Herbert. I hesitate to bring him up because poets and poetry are not terribly popular these days. I'm afraid their mere mention may cause your eyes to glaze over. But Herbert's thought on this vital theme is so valuable that I'm going to insist you meet him.

Herbert prayed a prayer that could be the prayer of any Christian who understands the power of the Incarnation to transform work into sacrament. It was,

> Teach me, my God and King,
> In all things Thee to see,
> And what I do in any thing,
> *To do it as for Thee* . . . . (emphasis mine)

He entitled this prayer/poem, "The Elixir," after the magic stone sought by the alchemists of his day. They believed that this stone, or elixir, could transform common metals into precious. The prayer, "as for Thee," is the elixir for work, said Herbert. It transforms common work into holy communion, because it bids the worker to look beyond what he does to the One who stands above and behind and within it all. For,

> A man that looks on glasse,
> On it may stay his eye;
> Or if he pleaseth, through it passe,
> And then the heav'n espie . . . .

Do all of your work as though you were doing it for the Lord. Then your work will become sacramental—a visible sign of an invisible reality. It will become a glass, a window, through which to see heaven.

> A servant with this clause
> Makes drudgerie divine:
> Who sweeps a room, as for thy laws,
> Makes that and th' action fine.
>
> This is the famous stone
> That turneth all to gold:
> For that which God doth touch and own
> Cannot for lesse be told.[3]

"*To do it as for Thee.*" Is that not the way God intended work to be done from the beginning? He made us stewards over his earth and charged us with the responsibility of managing it as he would—to do all our work as for him. When he made us stewards he was inviting us into a fellowship, a communion with him. Our work was to be one way we could meet him in the world.

To say Jesus saves our work is to say he restores it to what God made it to be before sin corrupted it. It is to say that the things we must do to live can become things we live to do. It is to say that mere jobs can become high callings. Why? Because, *that which God doth touch and own/Cannot for lesse be told.*

There is nothing more terrible than activity without insight.
Thomas Carlyle

4 ～

One Vocation, Many Occupations

"You can't eat for eight hours a day nor drink for eight hours a day nor make love for eight hours a day," said William Faulkner. "All you can do for eight hours is work. Which is the reason why man makes himself and everybody else so miserable and unhappy."

Maybe the reason we can get so confused and miserable about our work is that we spend too much time at it. But I doubt that is the reason. Thomas Carlyle came closer to the mark when he wrote, "There is nothing more terrible than activity without insight." For so many of us, our lives are filled with an excess of activity but little insight—especially in our work activity. We are asking, "What does it mean, this thing that I spend so much of my time doing?"

Vocation

The Scriptures give us the critical insight we need into the meaning of the activity of work. It's wrapped up in the word *vocation.* If we can understand what the Bible means by vocation—in contradistinction to what the world means by it—we will have the key that unlocks the door to meaningful and satisfying work Our work can become a way both to serve and to encounter God in the world. Mere jobs can become callings.

Our English word vocation comes from the Latin word *vocare,* which means "to call." A vocation is literally a calling. The New Testament word with the same meaning is the Greek noun, *klesis.* The biblical insight into the activity of our work is this: we are a called people. Called by whom? Called by God. Called to do what? Called to be his servants and priests in the world.

The most famous New Testament passage on this call, or vocation, is 1 Peter 2:9, "But you are a chosen people, a royal priesthood, a holy nation, a people belonging to God, that you may declare the wonderful deeds of him who *called* you out of darkness into his wonderful light" (italics mine).

We are a called people, a people of vocation. That is literally what the church, the Christian community, is. The Greek word for church is *ekklesia,* from *ek,* "out of," and *klesis,* "a calling." The church is the fellowship of the called. In the strictest sense of the word, the church is a vocational institution.

One Vocation, Many Occupations

If we are going to gain the Bible's insight into the activity of work we must begin with a clear distinction in our vocabulary. Contrary to the way the word is used in the world, the word *vocation* should refer to our calling to be God's people, his servants and priests in the world. We need the additional word, *occupation,* to refer to our work, or what the world means by vocation. Hence, we Christians can have many different occupations, but just one vocation. Individually, we may be stone masons, accountants, psychologists or auto parts salespersons in our occupations. But we are all, each of us, called to be servants of Jesus Christ in our vocation.

The Reformers, especially Luther and Calvin, gave much thought to the meaning of work under this theme of vocation. Their favorite biblical text was 1 Corinthians 7:17–24, where the apostle Paul seems to make the same distinction between vocation and occupation. But instead of two words, he uses just one to convey two meanings. In both cases he uses the Greek root word for call. But the sense of one is call with a small "c," or occupation; the sense of the other is Call with a big "C," or vocation.

Responding probably to questions from the Corinthian Christians about what they should do with their occupations now that they belong to Christ, Paul says, "Nevertheless, each one should retain the place in life that the Lord assigned to him and to which God has *called* him" (7:17, italics mine).

Note the way Paul speaks of their places in life as assigned to them by the Lord and as "callings" in a sense. He makes the same point in verse 24: "Brothers, each man, as responsible to God, should remain in the situation God *called* him to" (italics mine).

To be sure, not all of these "callings" Paul speaks of are occupational. For example, in this passage Paul describes also the stations in life of circumcised or uncircumcised as "callings." These are religious stations or "callings." One presumes that if the situation demanded it, Paul would speak of several other kinds of life situations as "callings," also. Occupation is but one kind of calling.

But these "callings" are not the same as our Calling in Christ. In verse 20, Paul uses a noun and a verb form of the same Greek word for call, but in these two different senses. The translators of the NIV render the noun form as "situation," or calling, with a small "c." The verb form comes across as Calling in the sense of the Call of God: "Each one should remain in the *situation* which he was in when God *called* him" (italics mine).

Here we have both senses of the word "call": occupation

and vocation. The Greek is literally, "each one in the calling in which he was called, in this let him remain." On the one hand, there are the situations or places in life which God has assigned to each of us—"callings," if you will. On the other hand there is our Calling in Christ.

Vocation over Occupation

Paul does a remarkable thing with the relationship between vocation and occupation, Calling and callings. He radically relativizes all occupations and life stations in the light of the Christian's vocation: "Were you a slave when you were called? Don't let it trouble you—although if you can gain your freedom, do so" (7:21).

Paul seems to be saying here: "Were you working the night shift at the parking lot when you were called? Do you hate your job? No big deal! If you get a chance to change jobs, go ahead and take it. But don't get so agitated trying to change your occupation that you lose sight of your vocation."

What really matters is not our occupations, but our vocation. Our vocation makes a janitor at corporate headquarters as good as the chairman of the board, and the chairman of the board no better than a janitor, since both belong to Christ. "For he who was a slave when he was called by the Lord is the Lord's freedman; similarly, he who was a free man when he was called is Christ's slave" (7:22).

One vocation, many occupations. But all of our occupations must be conducted under the authority of our vocation. Emily Post was once asked, "What is the correct procedure when one is invited to the White House and has a previous engagement?" She answered, "An invitation to lunch or dine at the White House is a command, and automatically cancels any other engagement."

Paul says much the same of our stations and situations in life: they are not cancelled by our vocation in Christ, but they are made of minor importance next to it. In fact, each "calling" must become a theatre in which to pursue our Calling or vocation as God's servants. Are you rich or poor, high or low? Are you a short order cook or an attorney, an artist or a gardener? No matter, for all that matters is to obey God's commands.

When John Wanamaker was Postmaster General of this country, he was very involved in running the Sunday school of his church. He was asked, "How do you get the time to run the Post Office and the Sunday school too?" He answered, "Why, the Sunday school is my business! All other things are just things. Forty-five years ago I decided that God's promise was sure: 'Seek first the Kingdom of God, and his righteousness; and all these things will be added unto you.'" There was a man who had his vocation in charge of his occupation, not the reverse.

One summer I met a physician from Portland. He had grown up in the Midwest and had attended the University of Chicago Medical School. So I asked him what made him choose Portland as a place to practice. I expected to get an answer having something to do with the beauty of the Pacific Northwest, the quality of living there or his wife's place of birth. His answer took me by surprise. He told me he had met a young seminary student while in Chicago and that this young man was going to go to Portland when he graduated and start a new church there for his denomination. He wanted to be a part of that kind of thing so he chose Portland as the place to be a doctor. Again, this was a man whose vocation called the shots for his occupation.

Vocation and Success

Who calls the shots for you? Does your vocation rule your occupation, or is it the other way around? Men in particular seem to have difficulty with this one. Their sense of worth as a man is usually predicated on how well they do in their work, not on how well they serve Christ. But a man could conceivably be a failure in his profession and a success in his vocation. Such are the men who keep their priorities straight and do not sacrifice their families for the sake of their jobs—or who refuse to do work that is immoral or dishonest. They may lose the job and win the vocation.

The prior importance of our vocation puts the success or failure of our various occupations in a brand new light. The sixteenth century Puritan, William Perkins, wrote a remarkable treatise on vocation in which he proposed that God may grant success to the work we do, not as a blessing, but as a test! Testing what? The purity of our sense of vocation. Were we pursuing our occupations and doing our work to selfishly feather our nests or to hear and obey God's call? How we handle success will tell. If we forget about the God who gave us the success, we can know we weren't serving our vocation in our work.

This isn't meant to cast a pall over whatever prosperity may come our way as we work—to rob us of whatever joy there is to be had for doing a good job and being rewarded for it in the here and now. It is meant to emphasize that our vocation is what stands over everything else and is finally all that matters. It is meant to elevate our vocation above all worldly measures of success and to place the final judgment of whether we did good or ill in the hands of God, not our accountant.

Contentedness

Our vocation urges us to cultivate the quality of contentedness in our occupations. Paul encouraged slaves not to worry about their occupations and to stay where they were— unless, of course, a golden opportunity presented itself to be free (1 Cor. 7:20, 21). He was saying, in effect, "Don't let restlessness and dissatisfaction in your job distract you from your calling to be God's man or woman where you are. Learn to be content in your work. Regardless of your situation, look for ways to be of service, in that situation, to your true Master, Jesus."

Controversy swirled around Richard Dent, defensive

end for the Chicago Bears, during the last weeks of the 1985/86 professional football season. He was very vocal about his dissatisfaction with his salary and demanded a new contract with higher pay. Even though he had been selected to play in the Pro Bowl and went on to be voted the Most Valuable Player in the Super Bowl, he was being paid "only" $90,000 a year. That was not nearly enough for a man of his immense talents, he argued, and it was making it difficult for him to give his best to the game. He said, "It's hard for a man to work when the pay isn't right."

That is true when you have no sense of vocation in your occupation. Salary isn't irrelevant, but it is a distant second place to the fulfillment of your vocation. As Phillips Brooks wrote, "Christianity helps us to face the music even when we don't like the tune." The tune may be sour—a less than desirable salary, a fool for a boss, difficult colleagues or poor working conditions. But one's sense of vocation will drown out the dissonance as the called individual looks for ways to serve Christ *in*, not *out* of the difficulty.

The apostle Paul wrote, "I have learned to be *content* whatever the circumstances. I know what it is to be in need, and I know what it is to have plenty. I have learned the secret of being content in any and every situation, whether well fed or hungry, whether living in plenty or in want. I can do everything through him who gives me strength" (Phil. 4:11b–13, italics mine).

None of this would have any credibility were it not for the fact that Paul writes these words from prison. In all the changes of life, Paul had one unifying theme: his vocation. He didn't try to negotiate a new contract with the Lord when the pay was bad!

My brother-in-law took his family to Zaire for two years. There he offered his skills as a carpenter to aid a remote mission station hospital. One of the problems of the hospital was inadequate sanitation facilities. When a Zairean goes to the hospital, the whole family comes along. On any given day, nearly 1,000 people can be in and around the hospital. There were only six outhouses and three flush toilets to service everyone. So Dan set out to build more. He also discovered that the existing outhouse pits were overflowing and needed to be pumped out. In one of his letters home he described how the mechanism overloaded when he began to pump out the accumulated human waste. It sent—how can I say this delicately?—human waste flying 30 feet into the air and splattering everyone within a radius of 20 feet!

Dan is definitely not being paid what he is worth! For just a few sentences later he will talk of the joy he has in the midst of the problems he has to put up with. He will thank God for the privilege of doing the thing God wants him to do at this time in his life. What's more, he will be embarrassed to read what I have said about him. Dan is no extraordinary Christian, he is simply a man of vocation who knows something of what it means to be contented in his work.

All this is not to say that we shouldn't improve our job situation if the opportunity is there. It is to say occupational dissatisfaction should not be allowed to rob us of vocational satisfaction in the midst of our jobs.

Obedience

Our vocation as servants of Christ also calls us to cultivate the quality of obedience in our occupations. Paul closes his passage on calling in 1 Corinthians 7 with the exhortation: "Brothers, each man, *as responsible to God,* should remain in the situation God called him to" (verse 24, italics mine).

Paul says our ultimate responsibility in our occupation—be it job or other station in life—is always to God, not whatever human is over us in the organizational chart. In Colossians 3:22–24, he tells slaves, of all people, to obey their earthly masters "in everything . . . . with sincerity of heart and reverence for the Lord. Whatever you do, work at it with all your heart, *as working for the Lord and not for men*" (italics mine).

This is not a call to the degradation of servility to an

earthly master. It is a call to the dignity and honor of service to the King of the universe. We serve the King through honest and diligent ministry to our earthly master. The master may take it as coming to him, but we will know that it is going to the Lord, through him. We may dislike our boss, but we can love our Lord by serving the one we hate—and along the way we may discover that we have learned to love our boss too!

A Christian has rights, but he or she always has duties before rights. In the New Testament, obedience and voluntary self-subordination are virtues. Perhaps it is here, more than any other place in Scripture, that we feel the gulf between our way of thinking (as twentieth century Americans) and God's way of thinking. The Greeks had not one positive word in their entire language for servant. Our Lord's call to be a servant, and Paul's instructions to the church, could not have been spoken into a more hostile culture. The Greeks are, in many ways, our cultural and philosophical forebears.

Another thing that is significant about these instructions is that they are given to slaves, without a word of condemnation for the institution of slavery. Christianity always focuses on the heart of the individual, not on a given system or institution. To be sure, in so doing it plants the seeds for the ultimate destruction of the system of slavery. But it starts with the premise that you will not have redeemed institutions until you have redeemed people.

The practical upshot is that our vocation in Christ would have us ask first what is wrong with us and our attitude before we say what is wrong with our jobs. It's too easy to set out to take the splinter out of the eye of the boss or the system and not to see the beam in our own eye. This is not a call to introspection and passivity in the face of oppression and injustice. It is a call to the most thoroughgoing confrontation with evil and injustice. It starts with its most impregnable sanctuary and fortress, our hearts, and works from there out into the world of systems and institutions. The chief measure of our redemption in our work is our willingness to be content and obedient in a difficult task, for the sake of our vocation to serve Christ through our job.

Dynamic, Not Static

The idea of one vocation in many occupations is dynamic, not static. It is protean in its adaptability to many different kinds of jobs and situations in life.

In the light of our vocation in Christ, Paul says our occupations are things we are to "walk" in. In 1 Corinthians 7:17, the word that is translated "retain" in the New International Version is really "walk," and reads literally, "Nevertheless, each one should *walk* in the place in life that the Lord has assigned to him and to which God has called him" (italics mine).

"Walk" is the very pictorial Jewish way of talking about the way our lives are lived. Lives are walks, movements in time, from birth to death. Our lives are stories, with beginnings and endings. Life is not static, it is dynamic. So is our vocation in Christ and the way it expresses itself in our occupations.

God's call is not something of which you can say, "I have answered it." It is something of which you must continually say, "I *am* answering it." Our vocation is certainly not something we discharge by choosing an occupation—teacher, businessman, lawyer, doctor, pastor—and then saying, "Well, I've done it, I've found my calling." Doing any one of these may be an act of obedience to our calling, for the present time; but it could be an act of disobedience later on!

God is a God of the future. He is always just one step ahead of us, out on the horizon, beckoning for us to follow, calling us on. The best definition of being a Christian I ever read was, "Giving what you know of yourself to what you know of God." The frontiers of both kinds of knowledge should be always advancing, as should the giving, the answering of God's call. All I would add to that is, "Being a Christian is giving what you know of yourself to what you know of God

in the situation in which you find yourself." The situation may
be social or political; it may have to do with your health or
marital status. It most certainly will have to do with your age!

The fluidity and dynamism of God's call does not wane
with the approach of old age. Theologian Karl Barth wrote a
lovely section on vocation in his monumental *Church Dogmatics* (he was in his sixties when he wrote it). He described
the horror of an old man and woman thinking that because
they are old they may now freeze in their vocation. He uses a
vivid image: "As if it were permissible to freeze or solidify at
the point where the river of responsibility should flow more
torrentially than ever in view of the approaching falls, of the
proximity of the coming Judge!"[1]

Just as a river speeds up its pace as it nears the precipice
of the falls, so old age is the time to really open up to God's
call! Why hold back and play it close to the vest when the time
is so short? How badly can you mess up your life when you
have so little left? What a contrast to the notion in our culture
that retirement is a time to reward yourself for all the work
you did in your youth by playing for the rest of your days. No
leisure world for the serious Christian!

Abraham and Sarah heard God's call when Abraham was
75 years old. Isaac was born to them when Abraham was 99.
He and Sarah had to deal with an adolescent in the household
when they were well into their hundreds!

Ludwig Van Beethoven was awakened in the night by the
sound of someone knocking insistently on his neighbor's door.
It was four raps, a pause, then four raps, a pause, then four
raps. The German composer could not go back to sleep, because those four raps became four beats that repeated themselves over and over again in his fertile musical mind. Thus
was the famous Fifth Symphony born, in which those four
beats repeat themselves with dazzling variety from the beginning to the end, always the same, yet ever new.

Our vocation is not static, but *dynamic*. It beats out its
claim on our lives in every situation, at every turn; ever the
same, yet ever new.

It is not what a man does that determines whether his work is sacred or secular, it is why he does it.

A. W. Tozer[1]

5 ~

New Reasons for Work

The late Ray Kroc, founder of the McDonald's hamburger chain, was once quoted as saying, "I speak of faith in McDonald's as if it were a religion. I believe in God, family and McDonald's—and in the office the order is reversed."[2] That kind of statement is, of course, anathema to the Christian concept of vocation, or Calling. No matter what our occupations are—musician, garbage collector, football coach— when we come to Christ we all become Christian workers first, musicians, garbage collectors or football coaches, second. Whatever our "callings," we are preeminently Called to serve Christ in and through our work.

At first sight, that outlook might seem to detract from the quality of work we do in our occupations. If everything must take second place to our vocation as Christian servants, then will not everything else be done in a second-rate fashion? Not so. In fact, a proper sense of vocation will have the opposite effect. A Christian whose vocation stands first may work as hard and as well as a Ray Kroc, perhaps better. The difference will be in his or her *motives*.

A young woman (who was a maid) had been converted to Jesus Christ and was applying for membership in the Baptist church pastored by Charles Spurgeon. The church had appointed a committee to examine all potential members. During the interview, Spurgeon asked her if there was any evidence that she had truly repented of her sins. She answered, "Now I don't sweep the dirt under the rugs in the house where I am employed." Spurgeon then turned to the others sitting on the committee and said, "It is enough. We will receive her."[3]

The young woman's sense of vocation had caused her to work better, not worse. For now she had a brand new set of reasons for work. What might they have been?

A Hidden Life

The apostle Paul lays down the foundation of Christian vocation in the third chapter of his letter to the Colossians: "Since, then, you have been raised with Christ, set your hearts on things above, where Christ is seated at the right hand of God. Set your minds on things above, not on earthly things. For you died, and *your life is now hidden with Christ in God*" (verses 1–3, italics mine).

Paul describes our lives as "hidden with Christ in God." The miracle and mystery of the Christian life is that when we trust in Christ we are born again. Our old life dies with Christ in his death, our new life is born with Christ in his resurrection. All that we are and ever will be is now "hidden" in Christ; he is our beginning and our end. Indeed, to use the words of Paul, he is our life.

I said that this is a miracle and a mystery. It is a miracle because new life in Christ is nothing any of us could will for ourselves, or bring about by our own efforts, or works. From first to last, it is a miraculous work of God. It is a mystery, because it defies human understanding. Who can comprehend how it can be that our true life is now hidden in Christ, with him as its beginning and end? But that is precisely the nature of the Christian life—union with him as our beginning and end and all that is in between.

An elderly Christian woman's memory began to slip. She had once known hundreds of memory verses, now all she could remember was one, 2 Timothy 1:12, "I know whom I have believed, and am convinced that he is able to guard what I have entrusted to him for that day." Little by little even that began to erode, until all she could remember was, "what I have entrusted to him for that day." Finally that too went, except for one word. The last weeks of her life all she would say over and over again was "him, him, him." She had nothing left of the Bible but that one word, but she had the whole of the Bible in that one word—and the whole of the Christian life. "Him, him, him;" that is the nature of our union with Christ.[4]

Union with Christ is also the root of all Christian ethics, including Christian work ethics. It begins with a comprehensive change in the way we believe and think about life. Note how Paul writes, "Since, then, you have been raised with Christ, *set your hearts on things above*, where Christ is seated at the right hand of God. *Set your minds on things above*, not on earthly things" (Col. 3:1, 2; italics mine).

G. K. Chesterton penned an unforgettable image of the theology of this text when he likened an unbeliever to a man born with his head stuck in the sand and his feet kicking in the air. To this man the things in the heavens seem airy and unsubstantial. The things of earth are all that are real. When you become a Christian, Chesterton wrote, God turns you right side up and places your feet on the ground, where they belong, and your head in the heavens, where it belongs. Now you can see clearly where to go and can walk where you see.[5]

This radical reorientation of our entire being, based on our union with Christ, causes us to walk and work differently upon the earth. It does not deny the reality of the earth or the things of earth. It just puts them in their proper perspective. There is a saying, "He is too heavenly minded to be any earthly good." The Bible's point of view is different. It teaches

that the only way to be of any earthly good is to be heavenly
minded. In fact, most of us are too earthly minded to be of any
earthly good.

The great seventeenth century priest George Herbert
was a poet of Christian vocation. The theme appears again
and again in his writing. In one poem he likens our life to a
medley, two tunes which are played together and interwoven; our life on earth and our life above. "Man," he says,

> "ties them both alone,
>   And makes them one,
> With th' one hand touching heav'n, with th' other earth."[6]

His best effort is a short piece he wrote on the passage
we've been examining, Colossians 3:3, entitled, "Our Life is
hid with Christ in God." He says life for the Christian "hath
. . . a double motion." That is, it is lived both on earth and in
heaven. Both are real and valid, but it is the life that is hidden
in Christ in heaven that is determinative for the life to be seen
in our daily labor. It is the invisible life that gives vitality to
the visible. He says of these two lives,

> Our life is wrapt in flesh, and tends to earth;
> The other winds toward Him, whose happie birth
> Taught me to live here that still one eye
> Should aim and shoot at that which is on high.[7]

The work we do proceeds from our "hidden" life in
Christ. That life may not be visible to the eye, but its impact
is plain for all to see in the work we do, which aims and shoots
"at that which is on high."

Witness for Christ

With this "hidden life" as his foundation, Paul then proceeds to build a structure of authentic Christian motivation in
work. He writes, "And whatever you do, whether in word or
deed, do it all in the *name* of the Lord Jesus, giving thanks to
God through him" (Col. 3:17, italics mine).

Do all your work "in the *name* of the Lord Jesus." That means that everything we do, including our work, is to be done in dependence on him, as his *servants* and *representatives* and *witnesses*. United to Christ, our lives hidden in him, we now bear the name of Christ. We are his people— Christians, Christ-ones. We must therefore carry his name honorably in our work.

Hudson Taylor said, "If your father and mother, your sister and brother, if the very cat and dog in the house, are not happier for you being a Christian, it is a question whether you really are."[8] Someone called this the "cat and dog test" of Christianity. There is also a "work test" for Christianity: "Is the place you work and the people with whom you work better and happier because you are a Christian?"

Paul wrote Timothy, "All who are under the yoke of slavery should consider their masters worthy of full respect, *so that God's name and our teaching may not be slandered*" (1 Tim. 6:1, italics mine).

He said the same thing to Titus: "Teach slaves to be subject to their masters in everything, to try to please them, not to talk back to them, and not to steal from them, but to show that they can be fully trusted, *so that in every way they will make the teaching about God our Savior attractive*" (Titus 2:9, italics mine).

Jesus taught that we, his followers, are the salt of the earth. Salt is a preservative; it keeps meat from going rotten. Our places of employment should be better places to work simply because we are there. But salt also makes people thirsty. The people with whom we work should be left with a thirst for Christ because they have worked with us and have seen how diligently and honestly we work and the respect we show others.

The Fear of Christ

A life hidden in Christ has new reasons, new motives for work. The desire to see the name of Christ exalted in the work we do is near the top of the list. But the fear of the Lord is number one. This most important motive is difficult to understand for us Americans living in the second half of the twentieth century.

One reason it's hard to understand is that it's even more difficult to swallow. Paul picks what for us is the worst, the most despicable kind of employment to make his point: slavery. He commands slaves, of all people, to obey their earthly masters as a way of obeying the Lord: "Slaves, obey your earthly masters in everything; and do it, not only when their eye is on you and to win their favor, but with sincerity of heart and reverence for the Lord. *Whatever you do, work at it with all your heart, as working for the Lord, not for men*" (Col. 3:22, 23, italics mine).

Furthermore, Paul commands slaves to obey their bosses as a way of showing to the Lord the tenderest and most holy of attitudes: fear. In the translation I just quoted, the New International Version, the word *fear* does not appear; *reverence* does. But the literal meaning of the Greek is fear. Modern translators have been a bit squeamish with this word. They apparently have a theological prejudice against fear as a legitimate motivator in the Christian life, so they substitute words like reverence and awe. These words aren't completely inaccurate, but they fail to capture the power of the word fear.

Fear is the word used throughout the Old and New Testaments to describe the terror and even panic a sinful person feels when brought into the presence of a holy God. It is the word that best describes Isaiah's reaction when he saw God in the Temple. It is the word that comes closest to what Paul experienced on the road to Damascus when he encountered the resurrected Christ. The word fear conveys the utter seriousness and gravity we should attach to our relationship with God. He is the Lord, we are his subjects. It is his to command, ours to obey.

As Abraham Kuyper put it, there is no area of life that the Lord Jesus Christ does not lay his hand on and say, "Mine!"[9] That includes our jobs. Since all of life is to be lived as service to the Lord, all we do in our work should be done with the fear of the Lord before us. All the earnestness and weight we attach to our relationship to him should be felt in our jobs. We know we stand before an awesome God who expects us to do all our work as unto him, and who will one day demand an accounting of what we did.

New Boss, New Diligence, New Holiness

This tells us three things about our work. First of all, if we are Christians, we have a new boss. It is not the person above us on the organizational chart. It is the Lord himself. As a way of serving God, we serve the person placed over us in the human organization.

Second, because our boss is really God, and we serve our earthly boss as a way of serving our heavenly Boss, we work sincerely and wholeheartedly—not to curry favor with our boss, but to please the Lord. "The conviction of the Christian workman," says William Barclay, "is that every single piece of work he produces must be good enough to show to God."[10]

In his book *Lyrics*, Oscar Hammerstein tells of the time he saw a picture of the top of the head of the Statue of Liberty, taken from a helicopter. He was amazed at the detail and painstaking work that was done on the lady's coiffure. Hammerstein reflected that the sculptor could not have imagined, even in his wildest dreams, that one day there would be a device that could look on the top of the head of his creation. Yet he gave as much care to that part of the statue as he did to the face, arms and legs. He wrote, "When you are creating a work of art, or any other kind of work, finish the job off perfectly. You never know when a helicopter, or some other instrument not at the moment invented, may come along and find you out."[11]

The Lord, not our earthly boss, is ultimately the one before whom we do our work. He sees each thing we do, big or small, hidden or revealed. Therefore all we do is to be done as unto him with great care and diligence.

Speaking of bosses, even the bosses have a boss! After Paul's words to slaves, he says briefly, but essentially, the same thing to masters. He reminds them to do for their slaves, "what is right and fair, because you know that you have a Master in heaven" (Col. 4:1).

Third, this word fear points to the essential sacredness of all the work that we do. Fear is the emotion of one who stands in God's holy presence. To work as unto the Lord is, by definition, to do a holy thing. There is no such thing as work that is, in itself, secular work. There are only two kinds of work: work done as unto Christ, and therefore sacred; or work done as unto whoever or whatever else, and therefore secular. I read of a sign kept over a kitchen sink: "Divine service is conducted here three times daily." The equivalent could be placed over a desk, word processor, workbench, or steering wheel.

Sharing in Christ's Sufferings

The apostle Peter brings to a breathtaking conclusion this view of the essential sacredness of all work done as unto the Lord. Work is perhaps never more sacred, says Peter, than when it is done under trying and difficult circumstances. Speaking to slaves who have cruel overseers, he urges them to submit to their masters and show respect. Why? Peter says working well at a bad job or for an evil boss can be a way of imitating Christ, of sharing in his sufferings. "If you suffer for doing good and you endure it, this is commendable before God. *To this you were called,* because Christ suffered for you, leaving you an example, *that you should follow in his steps*" (1 Peter 2:20b, 21, italics mine).

I told you this business about doing our work with the fear of the Lord before us was tough! Our most immediate impulse, when the boss, the money or the system begins to crowd in on us is to join singer Johnny Paycheck and tell all of the above to "take this job and shove it." But beyond the toughness, just the other side of it, is the joy of a special fellowship with Christ in his sufferings.

The cruel taskmaster need not be a boss. It may simply be the cards life has dealt you. To choose to do what you can, as unto Christ, will make even the most trying and degrading work holy.

I was moved and deeply impressed by the sign and picture I saw on a cardboard box in the foyer of a Baptist church in Minneapolis, Minnesota. The sign read, "Tim Lindbloom's Prayer Ministry." The picture was of a young man in a wheelchair, wearing a helmet—apparently the victim of cerebral palsy. There was a slot in the top of the box for people to insert prayer requests. There was also a note that said, "I only ask that you let me know what happens."

What work could this young man possibly do with his limitations? He could patiently endure and he could pray—especially pray. The only hints he might have that he was getting something done was to hear what had happened from those for whom he prayed—a special fellowship, and a special reward.

The Reward of Christ

Paul completes his structure of Christian motivation in work with a remark about the salary: "Whatever you do, work at it with all your heart, as working for the Lord, not for men, since you know that you *will receive an inheritance from the Lord as a reward*" (Col. 3:23, 24a, italics mine).

In union with Christ, our true life hidden in him, we not only have a new boss on the job, we also have a new source of income: an inheritance from the Lord as his reward for our work. In the Greek, the sense of the word, reward, combines the ideas of receiving what is our due and receiving it in full.

This future orientation of Christianity is a scandal to our age. We would rather work hard for a nicer home, a condo in the mountains, or a better car, than for the inheritance of the Lord. But it can set us free to labor in hope, diligent and joyful in a bad situation, when we are not appreciated and not paid what we are worth.

When John Calvin was banned from the ungrateful city

of Geneva, a city in which he had worked tirelessly and un-
selfishly for years, he said, "Most assuredly, if I had merely
served man, this would have been a poor recompense; but it is
my happiness that I have served Him who never fails to reward his servants to the full extent of His promise."[12]

A friend of mine secured a job for the summer when he
was in high school. It was a big disappointment; the pay was
low, the working conditions lousy. His dad asked him, "How's
the job going?"

He said, "OK, but I'm not getting paid enough money to
work hard."

His father's face turned livid with anger: "You said you
would work hard for what you got paid, so you will work hard
for it, no matter what they are paying you—or you will quit!"

That is a good lesson for a young man to learn about the
integrity of his word. There is only one thing I would add to
it: "You will work hard because you are working for the Lord
and he will pay you for what it was worth, and in full!"

Being set free to labor in hope means knowing that we
will be rewarded for our hard work. But it means more: it
means also that our hard work will somehow, by the grace of
God and the power of the resurrection, *matter*. After his
rhapsodic statement on the resurrection, in 1 Corinthians 15,
the apostle Paul draws his first practical conclusion: "Therefore, my dear brothers, stand firm. Let nothing move you.
Always give yourself fully to the work of the Lord, because
you know that *your labor in the Lord is not in vain*" (1 Cor.
15:58, italics mine).

The work of the Lord is above all preaching the gospel
and performing acts of mercy and justice in his name. But, as
we have seen from our text, it is also working wholeheartedly
at our jobs.

A tourist in Amsterdam visited the Church of St.
Nicholas. He had heard much about the beautiful chimes of
this cathedral and wanted to go up into the tower where they
were rung and see how it was done. He was shocked at what
he saw and heard there: there was a man standing before a

huge keyboard, wearing wooden gloves, perspiring and out of breath, pounding and thumping the keys. The noise was deafening—nothing but the rattle of the keys as they were pounded and the harsh dissonance of the bells clanging overhead. He left wondering why people thought the chimes were so lovely.

The next day he was sightseeing in another part of the city at the same hour. From across the city there came the most beautiful sound from the Church of St. Nicholas: the gentle music of the clear, full-toned bells. And he remembered the man in the tower and he hoped he knew how beautiful his hard work was in the distance.

We will never know the full significance of the work we did in our jobs "as unto the Lord" until we look back at them from eternity. All the work we did in Christ and for Christ will receive his reward, no matter how humble or unappreciated or unrecognized it may have been as it was being done.

There is something else about this gracious reward. It is way out of proportion to the work that any of us did or could ever do. Its premise, indeed the premise for everything that the Scriptures have to say about work, is the grace of God. The passage from which I have drawn most of my own conclusions about work begins with the phrase, "Since, then, you have been raised with Christ . . ." (Col. 3:1).

We don't work *so* we can be raised with Christ, we work *because* we have been raised with him! God's gift is not his response to the work we do; the work we do is a response to his gift!

I don't think I will be venturing too far if I say this: the same God who inspires in us the desire to work for him, will take the work we do (no matter how feeble and poorly motivated it was) and make it into something more than the thing it actually was when it left our hands. It is his grace from beginning to end. The great poet of vocation, George Herbert, said it well. The elixir that makes common things gold is the prayer, "as unto thee." But it is not our doing, it is God's,

> For that which God doth touch and own
> Cannot for less be told.[13]

Him, Him, Him

A hidden life. Witness for Christ. The fear of Christ. The reward of Christ. Are not these new reasons for work liberating and transforming and revolutionary? I am wrong on one count, however. There are not really *reasons* for work. There is but one reason for work: Him, him, him . . . . Jesus Christ, our Lord and boss, and the rewarder of those who serve him faithfully. Why do we work well and honestly and with respect for those we are serving? We work this way because of our union with him, our witness for him, our fear of him, and our hope for his reward.

Evangelist Sam Jones used to have what he called "quittin' meetings" for the new converts in his revivals. People would come and publicly confess their sins and repent of them. They would quit things like cussing, boozing, smoking and gossiping. He asked one woman what it was she planned to quit. She replied, "I ain't been doing nothing and I am going to quit that too."

To become a Christian is to quit doing nothing, even if it is working hard for a six-figure income. To become a Christian is to discover a brand-new job in the old one—and to start doing something there for the sake of the kingdom of God.

PART II

Someone to Love

> The grand essentials of happiness are:
> something to do, something to love
> and something to hope for.
>
> *Thomas Chalmers*

PROLOGUE II: ~

Someone to Love

"But I can't work that way!" The look on the man's face was a mixture of longing and helpless frustration. He had just heard me talk about the way we should see and do our work. But, as he put it, he was a realist. "All this stuff sounds beautiful. But I will leave the house tomorrow morning at 5:30. I will spend one hour on the freeway to get to work and another hour to get back. There is absolutely nothing I will do getting to work, working or getting home that bears the slightest resemblance to anything you or the Bible said."

He wanted to know how his occupation could be pressed into the service of his vocation. So many other voices were calling, Monday through Friday, nine to five. How could he hear Christ's call to serve him in and through his work? How could he even hear the beat of a different drummer, much less march to it?

Instead of liberation, all he saw was a heavier load to carry. It wasn't enough just to put in an honest day's work, I

seemed to be saying. I wanted him—no, God wanted him—
to glorify Christ, too, whatever that means.

A Perfectionist Husband?

Without one critical ingredient, all this talk about vocation in our occupation can sound like the perfectionist husband. No matter what his wife did for him, it never seemed to
be enough. At the beginning of each day he would make out
his list of chores for her to do, and at the end of each day he
would scrutinize it to be sure she did all she was supposed to
do. The best compliment she ever received was a disinter-
ested grunt if she finished everything. She grew to hate her
husband. When he died unexpectedly she was embarrassed
to admit to herself that she was relieved.

Within a year of her husband's death she met a warm
and loving man who was everything her former husband was
not. They fell deeply in love with each other and were mar-
ried. Every day they spent together seemed better than the
day before.

One afternoon as she was cleaning out boxes in the
attic, a crumpled piece of paper caught her eye. It was one
of the old chore lists her first husband used to make out for
her. In spite of her chagrin, she couldn't keep from reading
it again. To her shock and amazement she discovered that,
without even thinking about it, she was now doing for her
new husband all the things she used to hate to do for her old
husband. Her new husband had never once suggested that
she do any of those things, but she was doing them anyway—
because she loved him. Work that had been naked drudgery
had been clothed in love and was transformed into joyful
service.

The Critical Ingredient

The critical ingredient for vocation in our occupations is
love. It is love for God that clothes our work in joy. Work goes

sour when we lose personal, loving contact with the One for whom we were created to work.

The chief way our love for God is nurtured is in the practice of Christian worship. Most of us see worship as the thing we do to *express* our love for God. That is correct, as far as it goes. It is true that when we worship God we respond to his love for us by expressing our love for him in song and prayer and thanksgiving. But what is missing in this notion is the understanding that worship is also the activity, par excellence, through which God wants to *impress* his love upon us. Worship done as Jesus prescribed, in Spirit and in truth, is an encounter, a meeting with the true and living God. You and I cannot come away from a meeting like that and remain the same. As God impresses himself upon us in worship we are transformed, little by little, into his lovers. When that happens our work is changed, too—into a labor of love.

Thomas Chalmers was almost right. The first grand essential of happiness is something to do. The second is, not something, but *someone* to love. What is true of happiness in general is true of work in particular; to be joyful it needs love. Someone once said duty makes us do things well; but love makes us do them beautifully. Worship can turn duty into love and merely good work into a thing of beauty. Just why and how that is so is what we will be addressing in the next few chapters.

The glory of God is man fully alive and the life of man is the vision of God.

Irenaeus

6 ∼

Worship Is Forever

"You will understand when you get older."

Oh, how I hated to hear that patronizing statement from my parents when I was in junior high school! And it usually came after a protracted argument over what I wanted to do, as opposed to what they insisted that I do. It was the last attempt, on their part, to use reason to respond to my "But whys," before resorting to the old bottom line, "Because we said so, that's why."

One common situation in which this hated bromide appeared usually took place about 8:00 Sunday mornings. It was in response to my groggy protestations from my bed that I didn't see the need to go to worship that morning. Why couldn't I sleep in, get up when I was fully refreshed, shower and then read my Bible in the privacy of my own room? Wouldn't that be just as good? Wouldn't I learn just as much, and in half the time? After all, wasn't it you who taught me that it is faith in Christ as Savior and Lord, not church attendance, that made me a Christian? Isn't the true worship of God what we do for him in our everyday lives, anyway? What's the big deal? What's so important about going to an unimportant little worship service? My parents always responded with, "You'll understand when you are older."

They were right and I have to chuckle to myself as I write this chapter on the importance of worship. It is, in its own way, a testimony to just how right they were.

Worship Is Forever

Why is worship so important? More specifically, why is it so important to our work? The first reason is that, *of all the work we do, worship is the one work we will do forever.*

Did you notice that I called worship a work? Does it seem odd to you that these two words, work and worship, would be set beside each other? The truth is, these two words are so close to each other in their biblical meanings that their conjunction is actually redundant.

There is a wonderful and pregnant ambiguity in the Bible's words for work and worship: in both the Old and New Testaments the word for each is the same. In the Old Testament, the Hebrew *abad* can be translated either way—work or worship. Likewise, in the New Testament, the same Greek word, *leitourgein,* can either be translated liturgy, as in a service of worship, or it can be translated in purely secular terms, as in service to the king or service in the army. Only the context determines which meaning should be selected by the translator.

Worship and Work: Two Liturgies!

One word, two meanings. Or is there really just one? The dual use of the word suggests that faithful service to God is rendered no more in a church service than it is in a "work service"—if the work is done for God. In the Bible there is an indissoluble unity between worship and work, since both are forms of service to God. There is the service we render to God in our worship and there is the service we render to him in our work. The former is the liturgy of the sanctuary, the latter is the liturgy of the world.

But of the two forms of work—or worship, if you will—it is only the liturgy of the sanctuary that is eternal. Whatever you happen to be doing now from nine to five will one day pass away. The time will come when there will be no more need for housewives, certified public accountants, fry cooks, bus drivers, attorneys, engineers, bankers, carpenters, politicians, plumbers, tailors, teachers, auto mechanics and insurance salesmen. Even the work we do for the kingdom of God will outlive its usefulness. Evangelism will one day no longer be needed. Christian education will come to an end, as will prophecy and social services. But the work of worship will go on forever.

The best and the brightest in the eternal realms already know this. The apostle John's vision of heaven in the Book of Revelation is filled with scenes of worship. In chapter 4, for instance, there are four terrifyingly magnificent and wise creatures singing day and night, without ceasing, "Holy, holy, holy is the Lord God Almighty, who was, and is, and is to come!" (Rev. 4:8). All they do is worship God, forever and ever. Each time you turn a page in the Book of Revelation, you are looking at yet another scene of worship in heaven. Here it is the twenty-four elders, there it is ten thousand times ten thousand angels, here it is the martyred saints, and on and on.

The worship of God is forever. When we worship God we introduce a bit of eternity into our lives and work. That is why it is so important to our work. In heaven all the earthly work and worship we offered to God will be woven into a banner of eternal praise to God. It is the temporal work we did for the sake of eternity that will last. In heaven, the twin liturgies of the sanctuary and the world will come together in perfect unity forever.

Worship Transforms Work

"Is that all?" you ask. "Are you telling me that all we get for doing all that work and worship on earth is more worship in heaven?" Yes, I am—which leads to the second reason worship is so important to our work: *the work of worship transforms you, the worker.*

At first the thought of an eternal worship service disturbed me too, especially at 8:00 on Sunday mornings when I was arguing with my parents from under the bedcovers. As I read the Book of Revelation, heaven's endless worship service seemed like one long performance of Handel's *Messiah* (borrrring!)—performed by me and all the other poor souls who had to be awakened from death's sleep to be there.

When I expressed my misgivings to the youth director in my church, he assured me that I need not worry, since all those scenes of worship in heaven were "only" symbolic. His words were comforting. I took them to mean that whatever was going to happen in heaven was going to be a whole lot better than just singing the praises of God for all eternity. That reassurance held me through junior and senior high school, college, seminary and the first few years of my pastorate.

But lately I have been wondering if the citizens of heaven know something that I do not. C. S. Lewis suggested an analogy that opened me up to this possibility, and I give you my own version of it. Suppose I were to read one of Shakespeare's sonnets to my dog Pippin. Pippin is an ancient, deaf and indefatigably lascivious mutt, with nothing of the noble beast in him. Imagine his reaction as I begin to read him this piece from the great literary tradition of Western Civilization. At first he would wag his tail and look at me expectantly for scraps from the table. But after hearing the gibberish I was speaking he would lie down and go back to sleep. He's only a dog. He has no capacity to appreciate what is being read to him.

But what would it mean if, as I read to him, he perked

up his ears, looked at me with bright eyes, and barked his
approval? I could only conclude that something marvelous
and radical had happened to his nervous system, and that he
had been given the gift of appreciating fine literature.

Question: Would Shakespeare's sonnet be any better if
my dog could understand and appreciate it? No, of course
not. But would my mutt be any better? Yes, of course. Pippin's
appreciation of Shakespeare would not ennoble Shakespeare,
but it would ennoble Pippin!

Nothing More Delightful

What I was missing as a young teenager, and to a degree
continue to miss, is the capacity to so appreciate God that I
can think of nothing more delightful and interesting to do
than to sing my love and appreciation to him for eternity.
Those strange and wonderful beasts in Revelation have that
capacity. The elders and martyrs and angels have that capacity, but I do not . . . yet.

But someday I will when something happens to me that
the Bible calls being glorified. On the day that I meet Christ
face to face, I will be so renovated and expanded and fine-
tuned in my spirit that I will be able to fully appreciate God
as he is. St. John writes: "We know that when he appears we
shall be like him, for we shall see him as he is" (1 John 3:2).
That is what it means to be glorified: to be able to see him as
he is, because we have become as he is. On that great day,
as with Shakespeare and my mutt, God will not be any better
because I can perfectly appreciate and love him in all his
beauty and majesty. But *I* certainly will be better!

According to the Westminster Shorter Catechism, the
chief end of man is "to glorify God and enjoy him forever." As
C. S. Lewis observes, in heaven we will experience fully what
now we can only dimly anticipate in our worship: the truth
that these two things, glorify and enjoy, are one and the
same, because "fully to enjoy is to glorify. In commanding us
to glorify Him, God is inviting us to enjoy Him."[1]

I am not saying that heaven will be one long service of worship, at least in the manner that we now know. It may or may not be, I don't know. I suspect that heaven and its delights must be relegated to the class of things Paul wrote of: "No eye has seen, no ear has heard, no mind has conceived what God has prepared for those who love him" (1 Cor. 1:9). But my point is this: when we have been glorified, so as to be able to perfectly appreciate God, an eternal service of worship may not be all that bad. What could be more enjoyable than to have a clear, unimpeded and eternally uninterrupted gaze at the One who is beauty, wonder, truth, power, holiness, wisdom and love? Can you think of anything better?

At one time, all the Bible's commands to praise God left me with a picture of him standing around with his hands in his pockets fishing for compliments. But he doesn't need them—*we* need to give them. A popular Sister Corita poster of the 1970s was of church father Irenaeus's famous line, "The glory of God is man fully alive." We all loved that kind of stuff in the '70s. But what was missing was the remainder of Irenaeus's statement: "and the life of man is the vision of God." God is glorified as we come alive; and we come alive, are glorified ourselves, as we awaken to the vision of God in worship.

Priests, Then Kings

Worship transforms our work by transforming us, the workers. As we are changed to be more like the people God created us to be from the beginning, the work we do becomes more like the wonderful and fulfilling thing God intended it to be from the creation. In the beginning God gave us work to do as stewards of his creation. He set us over the world, but under him. It was only as his servants that we could be the earth's rulers. But when sin entered the picture, we and our work fell from this lofty place. When we ceased to be servants we also stopped being rulers. To return to the worship of of the true and living God is to be restored to the place we once were.

Poet George Herbert called man "the world's high priest." In a worship service, a priest is one who stands before God as the representative of the people in the congregation. He offers prayers to God in their behalf. Herbert is touching on a profound biblical truth when he says that you and I are to the world what a priest is to a congregation. We were appointed by God to act as representatives of the creation, giving words and voice to the praise that the mountains, seas, plants and animals cannot give. The man who does not praise God does not refuse "unto himself alone," said Herbert, but robs the whole creation, "And doth commit a world of sin in one."

It is only as we learn to worship well that we learn to work well. To worship God is to return to the place in creation where God created us to be. It is our priestly calling that makes our kingly position possible. Only as priests can we be kings! That is indeed what we are in Christ, "a *royal* priesthood" (1 Peter 2:9). As worshipers, our work can become a royal enterprise instead of a slavish drudgery. In worship the work of heaven touches the work of earth, and the liturgy of the sanctuary transforms the liturgy of the world.

A Reality Check

There is a third reason why worship, the liturgy of the sanctuary, is so important for work, the liturgy of the world. *The cultivation of the vision of God in worship sharpens our focus on what is real.*

Plato's famous analogy of the cave has helped me to think about this. Suppose a man is born in a cave and spends his entire life tied to a post, facing the wall at the rear of the cave. He cannot look to the right or the left, only forward. The light from the outside shines from behind him on the wall he faces. Occasionally people and animals walk by the cave's entrance and, as they do, their shadows are cast on the wall.

These shadows and the dim light on the wall are all he ever knows of reality. To him they *are* reality. To speak of a world outside the cave, made of color and three dimensions, would be incomprehensible to him.

To worship God is to take a peek at the world outside our cave. Our cave is the "world" that St. John speaks of in his gospel and epistles. By "world," John does not mean the creation. That is made by God and is good. It deserves our love and care. By "world," John means the evil world system of false values and human pride, implacably hostile to God and ruled by Satan, the "Father of Lies." John describes this "cave" as the "cravings of sinful man, the lust of his eyes and the boasting of what he has and does" (1 John 2:16). The "world," in this sense, is a spiritual cave.

The "world cave" is illusory and fading, but it exerts tremendous power over our hearts and minds. According to the New Testament, this "cave" is God's chief competitor for our beliefs and affections. It is to our souls what Plato's cave was to its inhabitant. Part of what it means to be redeemed by Christ is to walk no longer in darkness, but to be given the Light of the World. It is to begin to see things through God's eyes, as they really are.

Worship is a reality check. To cultivate the vision of God in worship is to gain glimpses of the Light in a world that lives in darkness. Such peeks are essential if we are to be able to navigate our way through the world. When God is worshiped our vision of reality is sharpened and we are enabled to walk and work without stumbling. When we worship God we are enlivened and envisioned to see the truth and to tell the difference between it and the lie.

The Symbolic Focus of All Our Work

The liturgy of the sanctuary is "the symbolic focus of all of our service to God," says theologian Geoffrey Wainwright. Our whole lives, everything we do in love, friendship, marriage and work, are to be lived as acts of worship. That's what

Paul meant when he told the Romans to offer their "bodies
as living sacrifices"—that being their "spiritual act of worship" (Rom. 12:1, 2). We are not "done" with worship when
we walk out of the church on Sunday morning. Every minute
of every day is to be a service of worship to God.

But it is precisely because our whole lives in the world
are to be liturgy, that the liturgy of the sanctuary is so critical. The liturgy of the sanctuary is to the liturgy of the world
what the cultivation of a garden is to the life and health of
that garden. The main business of a garden is simply to grow
and be a garden. That takes up most of its time. But, from
time to time, the garden is cultivated: watered, pruned and
fertilized—not every day, but regularly and often. A garden
left untended will go to seed; it is the cultivated garden that
is a thing of beauty. Work ceases to be worship if it is not
cultivated in specific, symbolic acts of worship, regularly and
often.

According to Wainwright, this cultivation of our work
through worship takes place in a two-way movement. One
movement is to start at the critical focal point of the liturgy of
the sanctuary and to move from there into the liturgy of the
world—the work we do the rest of the week. In the world,
the truth we saw and heard in the sanctuary must be translated into practical action in our work.

The other movement is in the opposite direction. It is to
bring back to the sanctuary the struggles and questions we
faced in the world as we tried to apply there what we saw and
heard in the sanctuary. Back in the sanctuary they can be
clarified, more sharply defined and even transformed.

Life in the "Real World"

I find nothing more irritating than talk among Christians
regarding the "real world." I usually hear it after a particularly captivating service of worship. Meaning to pay me a
compliment, someone will say, "That was a terrific service!
It's too bad we have to go back to the 'real world' now." The

assumption is that what happened in worship was a pleasant and therapeutic diversion. But the real thing is out there in the rough and tumble of the world.

Not so! What we saw and felt in worship is the "real thing"! The trick is to remember what we saw and felt when we go back into the world. It is in the light of this reality that we are to return to the world of lies and live the truth.

I know. A typical worship service on a typical Sunday in a typical church seems to be anything but heavenly. To be sure, our worship this side of heaven is always partial and fragmentary. But it participates now in what will be. C. S. Lewis borrows an image from John Donne, and describes worship as "tuning our instruments."

> The tuning of the orchestra can be itself delightful, but only to those who can, in some measure, however little, anticipate the symphony . . . . even our most sacred rites, as they occur in human experience, are, like the tuning, promise, not performance. Hence, like the tuning, they may have in them much duty and little delight; or none. But the duty exists for the delight. When we carry out our "religious" duties we are like people digging channels in a waterless land, in order that, when at last the water comes, it may find them ready. I mean, for the most part. There are happy moments, even now, when a trickle creeps along the dry beds; and happy souls to whom this happens often.[2]

Tuned to Hear and See

In worship we tune our spirits for the praise of God. We also tune our ears to hear him in the world.

It was the noon-hour rush on a steamy July day and the two men were pushing their way through the crowds in New York City's Times Square. They practically shouted as they tried to hear each other above the din. One man was a native New Yorker, the other was a Native American from Oklahoma.

The Indian stopped suddenly and said to his friend, "Listen! Can you hear the cricket?"

His friend was incredulous. "Are you kidding?" he laughed. "How could anyone hear a cricket in this bedlam!? You just think you heard it."

The Indian didn't argue. He just said, "Come over here and look." He walked over to a planter that was holding a large shrub, and pointed at the dead leaves in the bottom. To his amazement, the New Yorker saw a cricket.

"You must have an extraordinary pair of ears," he exclaimed.

"No better than yours. It just depends on what you are listening for. Watch this."

The Indian reached into his pocket and pulled out a handful of nickels, dimes and quarters. He then dropped them on the sidewalk. People everywhere stopped in their tracks and turned to look where the sound came from—some from as far as three blocks away!

"See what I mean?" he said. "It all depends on what you are listening for."

We have to recover a sense of God's presence in our work in the world. But we won't until we recover a sense of his presence in the work we do in the sanctuary. He is as present in the liturgy of the world as he is in the liturgy of the sanctuary, but it is in worship that we tune our spirits to hear and see him amid the noise and bustle of work.

Annie Dillard said it well: "The secret of seeing [or hearing!] is the pearl of great price. If I thought he could teach me to find it and keep it forever, I would stagger barefoot across a hundred deserts after any lunatic at all." But the trip is not that far. It may be only a few blocks away, at the place where you meet with other Christians to perform the Great Drama.

Holy, holy, holy is the Lord God Almighty,
who was, and is, and is to come.

Revelation 4:8

7 ~

The Great Drama

What do we do when we worship God?

We do pretty much the same thing I did last year when I watched, for the seventh or eighth time—I can't remember which—a video replay of the great 1974 University of Southern California/Notre Dame football game.

If you are unfamiliar with "sacred history," the game happened this way: At the half, Notre Dame was leading USC by a score of 27 to 14. But the game wasn't that close. From the way the Notre Dame team was pushing the USC players all over the field, the score should have been 54 to 0.

Ardent USC fan that I am, I was so depressed I almost didn't watch the second half. But I thought I would at least watch the kickoff, and if things continued in the same vein, I'd turn the set off and try to find something else to do to get my mind off the game.

Notre Dame kicked off to USC and Anthony Davis received the ball two yards into the end zone. (*O no, I thought. They're off to a bad start.*) Davis began to run up the middle of the field. Notre Dame tacklers were upon him almost immediately (I covered my face with my hands and peeked through my fingers). Davis faked his way past one, simply outran another, and then picked up a block from one of his teammates. Then he made a sharp cut toward the sideline and broke into the open field. In a moment he was in the clear and it was a footrace for the end zone, as one by one the Notre Dame defenders dove for Davis's body and legs and fell on their faces. I was on my feet screaming and pounding the back of my friend as Davis pranced into the end zone. The PAT was good, and suddenly the score was Notre Dame 27, USC 21.

Thus began the most electrifying second half of a football game I have ever witnessed. USC dominated Notre Dame and came back to win the game 55 to 27! Yippee! I feel good all over even now as I write about it.

Ritual Drama

If you are a Notre Dame fan, or if you are one of those who thinks football is the most trivial of pursuits, don't let what I have just written get in the way of the point I want to make: when you worship God you do pretty much the same thing I did when I watched that game on video for the seventh or eighth time. That game for me is a *ritual drama.*[1]

By *ritual* I mean a *fixed form of words and actions and symbols.* The word "form" in this definition is very important, for a ritual does not have to be exactly the same words and actions and symbols from moment to moment, just the same *kind.* In the case of the football game I just regaled you with, any USC victory over Notre Dame will do for the drama to qualify as ritual.

By *drama,* I do not necessarily mean drama in the sense of the spectacular, but drama in the sense of the *telling of a story.* A ritual drama, therefore, is a story told through the means of a fixed form of words, actions and symbols. The exact way the story is told may very well change with each telling, but the basic outline of the story must remain the same for the drama to qualify as ritual. As I said, any old USC victory over Notre Dame will qualify as ritual drama for me.

You need to know one last and crucial thing about ritual drama. The story is told for a purpose: to *extol and affirm and confirm the values and convictions* of the person or people to whom it is told. Whenever I tell someone how many times I have watched the 1974 USC/Notre Dame game, I usually hear this protest: "But you know how the game will turn out. Why do you watch it over and over?" My response is, "That is precisely the reason I watch it over and over—I know how it is going to turn out." I watch it because it embodies in story form a certain set of values and convictions I have about sports. These, admittedly, are trivial in nature but they are nevertheless things that I hold as worthy of at least a low level of praise. Also I enjoy the opportunity to see and hear them praised and to praise them myself as the story is told once more.

The Lion and the Lamb

The Bible is loaded with examples of worship as a ritual drama. One of the most vivid is found in a scene of worship in heaven, described in the Book of Revelation, chapter 5. The setting is extremely important. God is seated on his throne, surrounded by the congregation of heaven: twenty-four elders, four bizarre and magnificent creatures, and myriads upon myriads of angels. In his right hand is a scroll, written on the inside and the outside, as full of writing as it can possibly be, and sealed with seven seals. This scroll contains God's decrees—what he is going to do on earth.

Of course, everyone in heaven wants to see the scroll opened. For when that happens God's purposes will be unleashed. In a loud voice an angel asks what is on everyone's mind: "Who is worthy to break the seals and open the scroll?" The apostle John, who is describing this scene for us, looks around to see who it will be. But there is no one anywhere, not one. If the scroll cannot be opened, then God's good and righteous purposes cannot be put into effect! John is devastated. He writes, "I wept and wept because no one was found who was worthy to open the scroll or look inside."

Then one of the twenty-four elders speaks to John and says, "Do not weep! See, the Lion of the tribe of Judah, the Root of David, has triumphed. He is able to open the scroll and its seven seals." Ah, of course! The Lion is the One who can perform this mighty act. The Lion, who is the symbol of kingship and power and regality—*He* can open the scroll. In one of the most dramatic moments in Scripture, all heaven stands on tiptoe, poised, waiting for the entrance of the Lion. But instead, a Lamb appears, "looking as if it had been slain." The Lion is announced, but the Lamb enters. Who is the one with power and dominion and authority? The One who is the embodiment of sacrifice and service and humility. The Lamb is really a Lion. Could there possibly be a better picture of the mystery of Jesus Christ?[2]

Ritual Drama in Heaven

At this point, heaven breaks into a service of worship, and, as the congregation sings, a ritual drama unfolds:

You are worthy to take the scroll
  and to open its seals,
because you were slain,
  and with your blood you purchased men for God
  from every tribe and language and people and nation.
You have made them to be a kingdom and priests to
  serve our God,
and they will reign on earth.

(Rev. 5:9, 10)

Note the ritual. There is the singing of a hymn: a fixed form of words and actions. Note also the drama. The story of the gospel is told in outline: everything essential to the Christian story is here in capsule—past, present and future.

Christ is worthy to take the scroll and to open its seals because of the things he has done, is doing and will do. He was slain and has bought us with his blood; we are now, by his graciousness, a kingdom of priests called to serve our God; and we will, one day, reign on earth.

The telling of the gospel story becomes the occasion for an eruption of praise from not only every creature in heaven, but also from all creatures "on earth and under the earth and on the sea, and all that is in them . . . ." They sing,

> Worthy is the Lamb that was slain,
> to receive power and wealth and wisdom and strength
> and honor and glory and praise! . . .
>
> To him who sits on the throne and to the Lamb
> be praise and honor and glory and power,
> for ever and ever!
>
> (Rev. 5:12, 13b)

The Audience and His Performers

That hymn and what follows is a paradigm of biblical worship. All the discrete acts of worship: the singing of hymns, the reading of Scripture and the preaching of God's Word, the saying of creeds, the offering of prayers and thanksgiving, the giving of tithes, the praise of God and the celebration of the Sacraments—all these together *presuppose* and, in one way or another, *proclaim* the story of what God has done, is doing and will do. In the telling of the story of God's marvelous saving acts, he is thanked, praised and adored. In short, *in the telling of the story God is worshiped.*

Question: In the scene from the Book of Revelation that was just described, who is performing the great ritual drama and before whom is it being performed? Stop for a moment and reread the story. Then ask yourself: Who is the *performer* and who is the *audience* in this heavenly service of worship? The performer is the congregation of heaven, and the audience is God.

The Danish philosopher Sören Kierkegaard used a little aphorism to sum up volumes of sound biblical theology regarding worship. Paraphrased, it is: In Christian worship *God is the audience, the congregation is the performer, and those who stand up front and lead* (the preachers, readers and singers) *are the prompters.*

Unconscious Blasphemy

All this is to say that God is the focus of authentic Christian worship. He stands at the center, not we and our experience.

But stand with me outside a typical church on a typical Sunday. Look at the people walking into the church building. Think about their expectations as they walk inside to worship. Who do you think these typical churchgoers believe is the audience? The performer(s)?

The answer is easy, isn't it? They think they are the audience; and the preacher, choir, and others who lead from the front are the performers. And where does God fit into this scheme? I'm not sure, and neither are they. Perhaps he is there to perform. Perhaps he is there only as the owner of the building, watching the service from the back. Whatever the case, the congregation has gathered as an audience to enjoy a performance put on by preacher and choir.

By making themselves the audience, they have presumed to occupy the place in worship that is reserved for God alone. The Bible's word for this kind of role reversal is blasphemy, the deadliest of all sins. Much of what passes for worship in Christian congregations these days is really the most subtle and pernicious form of blasphemy: subtle because it looks and feels like worship, pernicious because it is the opposite.

Listening as Performance

But what about the sermon? That's the most frequent objection I hear to what I have just said. "I can see what you mean when it comes to singing and praying, but what about listening to a sermon? Isn't that a case of me legitimately being part of an audience listening to someone perform?" In the strictest sense of the word that is true. When you listen to a sermon you are an audience. But the *way* you listen should be thought of as a performance. Listening is not passive. To hear is not to receive a message as a cup receives coffee. To hear is to engage the speaker and what he says. Even if you say nothing at all, to hear is to enter into a kind of internal dialogue with the speaker. This is true of anything that is heard, from the ring of a telephone to the sound of a child's cry. How much more is it true of the hearing of the Word of God in a sermon!

To mix the metaphor with one used by the apostle James, "hearing" the Word of God is like looking into a mirror to see your reflection. You should pay such rapt attention to what you see there that you don't walk away and forget what you saw. Kierkegaard said that most people come to the mirror of God's Word only to measure it and study its properties but never to look in it! They can tell you everything about the mirror, but nothing about the person they should have seen there. To truly hear the Word of God, said Kierkegaard, is to say over and over again to yourself, "It is talking about me, and it is talking to me."[3]

How Did I Do?

Nothing can kill the effectiveness of a sermon faster than listening with a view to see how the preacher is doing. Even if he is brilliant, what is then noticed is he and his brilliance, not the word God wants to say to you. Listening is itself a kind of performance. God judges us on how we listen! The question after a sermon is not, "How did the *preacher* do?" but, "How did *I* do?"

God wrote the drama of our salvation. He produces and directs it. It stars his Son. It is the greatest story ever told because it tells us of the love and majesty of the One who rescued us from death and darkness and brought us into life and light. Even now he nurtures us by his Spirit and sustains us in the hope of his return. To worship him is to perform that drama before him in adoration and wonder.

"How did I do?" That's a performer's question. It's also a worshiper's question. It is motivated by a desire to please the author and hero of the drama of salvation. "How did I do?" That question applies even when we come to worship beaten down by the world, dried up inside, cold toward God, and generally hurting. When I come to worship in this state of mind it is easy to fall into an attitude that says to God, "Here I am, empty. Please fill me up."

It is true that God wants to fill us up when we are empty, and it is legitimate to ask him to. But if that is the extent of our prayer, then we will probably be disappointed when the service is over. What is needed is the additional prayer: "Now that I have asked you to fill me, Lord, please, by your Spirit, *set me free to forget myself and lose myself in adoration and thanksgiving.*"

Our Lord's healing paradox was that we find ourselves when we lose ourselves for him. We are filled when we are empty. We receive when we let go. This is never more true than it is in worship. We come to worship, needing desperately to receive something from God. We worship, we perform the ritual drama with God's people, offering to him what little we have to give, giving even what we do not have. We cease to ask, "What will he do for me?" and seek to ask, "What can I do for him?" My experience has been that God is marvelously generous in blessing people who will let go of their need to be blessed in order to worship.

Self-forgetfulness in Worship

Self-forgetfulness is the goal of all truly Christian worship. C. S. Lewis said the greatest test of being in the presence of God is that you either regard yourself as a small, dirty object, or you forget about yourself altogether. He added that, of the two, it is better to forget about yourself altogether.[4]

I would add that one follows the other. The intense and shattering self-awareness that comes with a deep sense of our sinfulness can be replaced by a liberating self-forgetfulness when we know our sins are forgiven. At first all we can see is how bad we are. But then all we can see is how good God is: the goal of all true worship. It is then we discover the truth of the Westminster Confession: that the chief end of man is to glorify God and to enjoy him forever; and that the two, glorify and enjoy, really do go together. The call to glorify God in worship is actually an invitation to enjoy him to the fullest.[5]

Because worship is a ritual drama in which God is the audience and we are the performers, it is only proper that we should ask, "How did I do?" A good performer does not ask, "What did I get out of that?" Instead, he or she wants to know if the performance measured up to its maximum potential and was the audience pleased.

Self-forgetfulness in Work

Self-forgetfulness is the goal for the service of worship. It is also the goal for the service of work. Remember how the two—worship and work—fit together. The same word in the Old Testament, *abad,* and the same word in the New Testament, *leitourgein,* can be translated either worship or work, depending upon the context.

Both worship and work are forms of service to God. Worship is the liturgy of the sanctuary. Work is the liturgy of the world. But it is the liturgy of the sanctuary that provides the pattern for the liturgy of the world. The same kind of self-forgetful love, adoration and gratitude that is the goal of all true worship should be the pattern for all work which is truly Christian.

So, a good worker, like a good worshiper, is one who forgets himself in the doing of the work. You and I should ask two questions of the work we do. The first is, "Is this work doing something that God wants done?" If the answer to that question is Yes, then the second question should be, "How can I give myself to this work, 100 percent, as I do it?"

Serve God by Serving Your Work

Dorothy Sayers said rightly that "The only Christian work is good work well done." If the work is good work, then it only follows that it ought to be well done. That being true, Sayers concludes, "the worker's first duty is to serve the work." Once you are satisfied that the work you are doing is work that God wants done, then the best way to serve God in your work is to *serve your work*—100 percent![6]

Sayers reflected on the fact that Jesus was a carpenter most of his adult life. She wrote, "No crooked table-legs or ill-fitting drawers ever, I dare swear, came out of the carpenter's shop at Nazareth. Nor, if they did, could anyone believe that they were made by the same hand that made heaven and earth."[7]

Jesus didn't wait until he left his carpenter's trade to serve God by preaching the gospel and healing the sick. He served God both in his carpenter's trade and in his preaching and healing. There was not a secular period in his life followed by a sacred period. All he did was sacred. All his life was a service to God—his worship and his work, his preaching and his carpentry.

The unity of the two, worship and work, requires that our work should demand from us the same self-forgetful service called for in our worship. When work is done this way it can actually feed back into our worship and make it better.

Serve God in Your Work!

Simone Weil wrote an essay with the unlikely title, "Reflection on the Right Use of School Studies with a View to the Love of God." She defined prayer as simply giving to God our uninterrupted, undivided, complete and rapt attention. She then said that school work should be done the same way; our studies should also receive our uninterrupted, undivided, complete and rapt attention. Why? Because the increased ability to pay attention can then be brought back to prayer, and make prayer better.[8]

The only thing I would add to what Weil said is that the attention paid in class or on the job is itself a form of attention paid to God. This is not to say that the work is God. Rather, it says that if the work is worth doing at all, it is worth doing the way the apostle Paul said everything was to be done: "with all your heart, as working for the Lord, not for men . . ." (Col. 3:23).

The Jewish philosopher, Martin Buber, tells the story of a Hasidic rabbi who received a complaint from one of the more pious members of his congregation. The distraught member came to report that certain Jews were staying up all night playing cards. He was perplexed when the rabbi smiled and said, "That's good. They are learning great concentration and becoming skilled at remaining awake for long hours. When they finally turn to God, see what excellent servants they will make for him." Worship feeds work; and work, thus nourished, feeds worship.[9]

All life is sacred for the Christian. Everything we do, big or small, significant or insignificant, is to be done as service to God. To use the metaphor with which I began this chapter, we are all performers of the great drama of God's love and salvation, in all areas of life—both in the sanctuary and in the world. A good performer has a singular focus. His focus is first on his art, only secondarily or indirectly on himself. Be it the violin or voice or acting—Beethoven, Tchaikovsky or Shakespeare—the great artist is first a servant. He becomes great only as he seeks the greatness of someone or something greater. Then greatness comes as a by-product, even a surprise. In all that we do, in our worship and in our work, it is always as our Lord promised: the first becomes last and the last becomes first.

It's true, this idea of work is at odds with everything we are being told today about the meaning of work. For instance, we are being told that the purpose of work is to get ahead in the race and make as much money as we can. Or we are told that we are to choose a career as a means of self-expression. Both notions are foreign to the Bible because they place us and our ambition at the center of work, not Christ and his kingdom. I am appalled at the number of men and women I meet—many of them Christians—who have absolutely no loyalty to their employers, beyond doing the bare minimum of work they agreed upon for the pay they are receiving. Listen! If the work our employers are paying us to do is good, then they deserve our complete loyalty as we do it. They deserve our maximum, not our minimum. The work should be a form of worship—not of the work, but of the God we serve through the work.

Everything, Everything, Everything!

Arturo Toscanini had just finished conducting a brilliant performance of Beethoven's Fifth Symphony. There was a moment of stunned silence, and then, as though one person, the audience rose to its feet and applauded and shouted its approval. Toscanini waved his arms violently for it all to stop. He turned to the orchestra and shouted hoarsely, "You are nothing!" He pointed to himself and shouted, "I am nothing!" Then he shouted, "Beethoven is everything, everything, everything."

That's the way it is with us and God: we are nothing, and he is everything, everything, everything! In our worship and our work, it is the beginning of wisdom to realize this. If we really believe this and order our worship and work accordingly, there is a surprise waiting for us. Like Toscanini, we will discover that we have performed brilliantly and have become great.

A man that looks on glasse.
On it may stay his eye;
Or if he pleaseth, through it passe,
And then the heav'n espie.

George Herbert[1]

8 ~

A Story within a Story

More is going on around us than we can ever know.

I can vividly remember the moment I became a Christian. Only nine years old, I was kneeling at a bedside covered with a blue and white floral bedspread. Beside me was my sister who was making the same decision. Across from us, kneeling at the other side of the bed, was Mrs. Dalton, our "Good News Club" leader. She was a white-haired little lady filled with the love of Christ, the patience of Job and the dogged determination of Balaam's Ass. For nearly a year she had persisted with inviting me to her home to hear the gospel story, and now I was finally responding to it in faith.

I saw only three people in that room, but there were far more. Jesus said that when one sinner repents, the angels in heaven rejoice. Although I couldn't see or hear them, creatures of vast intelligence and beauty were leaning over my little shoulders and shouting their approval.

More was happening than I could have ever known.

A Larger Reality

That is the way it usually is: in each moment of our lives there is more happening than we can know. If secularism says nothing means anything, Christianity says everything means everything. Paul says our battle here is not against just flesh and blood, but against powers and principalities, and rulers in the heavenly realms. There is not one square inch of neutral territory in the universe: everything is being fought over by God and Satan. Everything we do that we can see is part of a larger reality which we cannot see.

More is always happening than we know. That is certainly true in the worship of God. Every service we conduct is a tiny part of an eternal, magnificent and gigantic service taking place continuously in heaven. Every time we worship we join ten thousand times ten thousand angels in the adoration of God: every hymn we sing, every prayer we pray is part of something unimaginably lovelier, bigger and richer than the thing we do.

In the Book of Revelation we get peeks into this larger, heavenly reality. What stands out about worship there is that it is conducted as a drama, a story. God is praised and thanked for what he has done, is doing and will do. There is a history assumed and celebrated in worship: it springs from what has happened, what is happening and what will happen.

Of course! Our faith is in a gospel. Gospel means good news. News is about events, it tells a story. What saves us is not a set of ideas, but a series of events in history, centered around the life, death, resurrection and promised return of Jesus of Nazareth, Messiah and Son of God.

Note again how this good news is celebrated in verses 9 and 10 of Revelation 5, taken from the scene of heavenly worship we looked at in the last chapter:

You are worthy to take the scroll
    and to open its seals,
because you were slain,

and with your blood you purchased men for God
from every tribe and language and people and nation.
You have made them to be a kingdom and priests to
    serve our God,
and they will reign on earth.

The whole story of salvation is captured in that hymn of praise. God is celebrated for what he *did* in the past: "you were slain, and . . . you purchased men for God . . . ." He is worshiped for what he *is doing* now: "You have made them to be a kingdom and priests to serve our God, . . ." And he is praised for what he *will do:* "and they shall reign on earth."

"Playing" the Truth

Christian worship celebrates and stages a great Story, a cosmic Drama. In classic and Elizabethan drama the stage was regarded as a mirror of reality, a reflection of the larger reality outside that surrounded it. The performance was definitely not looked upon as an escape from the truth of the "real world"; it was, rather, a place where truth was focused for a while in order to somehow illumine the lives of those in the audience.

As with the Elizabethan stage, the Story we perform and remember on Sunday morning mirrors the transcendent reality of the great Drama God is unfolding in history. When we worship we "play the truth" for a while so we can better live it in the world.

"Play" the truth? Yes. Does that sound frivolous? Let me explain.

In the summer of 1985 I took my children to see the Walt Disney animated feature, *The Black Cauldron.* It was a poor adaptation of Lloyd Alexander's fine series on the Kingdom of Prydain, but the animation was terrific and my children were captivated by the story. For weeks afterward, they daily improvised costumes, fashioned swords out of sticks and played "Black Cauldron." The drama my children saw on the screen was so vivid, so compelling, so larger-than-life, i.e., transcendent, that they wanted to "play" it.

As many have observed—some of them even theologians!—the play of children is not frivolous. It is done with great seriousness. Any parent who has ever listened to the hot arguments that take place among children at play will attest to this. The arguments are usually over the "rules of the game," issues of protocol and the correct interpretation of what is being played and who gets to play whom. It is tremendously important to children that the game be played "right," and that he or she gets to be the character he or she wants to be.

In a very real sense, when children play, they are both actors and worshipers. Their games are plays in which they take on the roles in a drama that has captured their imaginations. They are also little services of worship in that they pay homage to the "truth" of the game or fantasy.

That's the sense in which we "play" in worship. We tell the Story again and again, we play the parts of the main characters, and as we do so we pay our homage; we worship the God of the gospel.

Rabbi Abraham Heschel was once confronted with a complaint from his congregation. Some of the members of the synagogue told him that the liturgy did not express what they felt. Would he please change it? Heschel wisely told them that it was not for the liturgy to express what they felt, it was for them to learn to feel what the liturgy expressed. As Jews they were to learn the drama and say it and "play" it over and over again until it captured their imagination and they assimilated it into the deepest places in their hearts. Then, and only then, would it be possible for them to live properly their own individual dramas.[2]

Stories within a Story

How much more should we Christians learn to "play" the Drama of our salvation each Sunday in worship. To do so is to learn to live our lives, our individual dramas, in its light. All other stories have an ending, each of ours included. The only story that will last is the Story of Him who was and is and is to come. The eternal Drama, the heavenly reality, is of the One who was slain, and by his blood ransomed men and women for God from every tribe and language and nation, and made them a kingdom and priests to serve God. Our stories find meaning only within that Story, as reflections of it. They endure only as they enter into it—as stories within a Story.

When we play the Story in worship we are reminded that each of our lives—our stories—are to be lived within God's great Story of salvation and hope. But much more happens than just a reminder. As the Story is performed, its reality breaks into our stories, our lives, and transforms them.

There is a delightful Hasidic tale about the power of stories. Whenever the people of the great Rabbi Israel Baal Shem Tov were in great danger, the good rabbi would go to a particular place in the forest to meditate. There he would light a fire and say a special prayer. Whenever he did this, a miracle would happen and his people would be saved.

A generation later, when the people of his disciple, Magid of Mezritch, were faced with a crisis, Magid would emulate his master. But he had forgotten how to light a fire. So he would just go to the same spot in the forest and say the prayer his master had taught him. And God would perform a miracle for his people.

Another generation later, the people of the Rabbi Moshe-Leib of Sasov were faced with a crisis. The rabbi did not know how to light the fire, and he had forgotten the prayer. All he could remember was the place in the forest. So he simply went to the place and, as he had hoped, God delivered his people from danger.

The rabbi of the next generation, Israel of Rizhyn, did not know how to light the fire, did not know the prayer, and had no idea where the place in the forest was. But when his people were in great danger, he would sit in his armchair and tell the story of what had happened to his ancestors. And that was sufficient to save his people.[3]

The telling of the Story, the acting out of the Drama of God's mighty acts, is sufficient. When celebrated in faith, the

Story is God's chosen way to bring light and healing and encouragement to us. For when we believe the gospel Story, the Bible says, we are, in some mystical way, "in" Christ: his death becomes our death to sin, his resurrection becomes our resurrection to new life, and his promised return becomes our hope. In short, his Story becomes our story.

The Story in Our Work

What does all this have to do with our work? What does the liturgy of the sanctuary tell us about the liturgy of the world? Can the Story we "played" in worship on Sunday transform the stories we live out in our work Monday through Friday?

It can. For one thing, the Great Story we proclaim and celebrate in worship gives the frame, or broader context, our work needs to have meaning. In worship, we are reminded that each of our stories is part of a larger Story written, directed and produced by God, and in which the lead is played by Jesus Christ.

Relax and Play!

We can therefore relax in our work. We have a part to play in God's great Story, but only a part; there is nothing we can do that will have any impact whatever on its outcome. The Great Story tells us that, compared to its grand sweep, all you and I can do is pitifully small and, in itself, insignificant. Our jobs and lives—our stories—only find meaning as they are touched by God and incorporated into his Story.

That insight should not discourage us, it should encourage us. Everything is not resting on our frail shoulders; in fact, very little is. God is in charge, not we. Martin Luther used to take comfort in the fact that he could stop working for a while, sit down, and enjoy a stein of Wittenberg beer, and rest in the peace that the Kingdom of God was marching on without his efforts!

Poet George Herbert would sometimes go to bed at night, groaning over how little he had accomplished during the day. Looking back over the day, all the work he did seemed to him to be no more than "foam . . . bubbles, balls of wind." Do you ever feel that way? Yet the poet could close his eyes and rest, knowing that God said to him,

> It doth suffice:
> Henceforth repose, your work is done.[4]

No matter, God is gracious, and he will accomplish what good we so feebly attempt and so often fail to achieve during the day. We can rest because not one moment of our day passed outside of his sovereign love and care. So Herbert writes,

> My God, Thou art all love:
> Not one poor minute 'scapes Thy breast,
> But brings a favor from above;
> And in this love, more than in bed, I rest.[5]

There ought to be a kind of playfulness about our work—not the escapist frivolity of so much that passes itself off as play these days, but the serious, earnest fun of children imitating their Heavenly Father. He has given us the gift of work. We may play at God as we go about our daily tasks, but we don't have to actually *be* God. Like children playing Star Wars, we can quit at lunch, go inside and eat our sandwiches and soup. We can go to bed at night knowing Dad will take care of us.

The future of the universe and the Rebel Alliance doesn't really depend on us. To be sure, God invests our work with real significance but, in the final analysis, it is what he does with our work, not what we did, that counts. The holy playfulness of worship is meant to make our work more playful.

Rescuing the Humdrum

The Great Story we celebrate in worship, and that frames our work, rescues the humdrum from insignificance. Sitting on a clogged freeway, functioning as a tiny cog in a big corporate machine, or standing in an unemployment line can make work seem pointless. But the Great Story says to us that this mess makes perfect sense to the Writer, Producer and Director of the story—and to his Leading Man. Even though we can't see how what we are facing fits in with the plot of the Story, he does. We can bear down and do the seemingly trivial, knowing that he does all things well and makes everything fit into his great design.

Trusting can open us up to meet God in the humdrum. Professor Belden C. Lane makes this point luminously in an article entitled, "Stalking the Snow Leopard: A Reflection on Work."[6] *The Snow Leopard* is the title of a book written in 1973, after writer Peter Mathiessen accompanied biologist George Schaller on a trek across the Himalayas to study the behavior of the Himalayan blue sheep. That was the "official" purpose of the expedition. The real purpose was the possibility of seeing the rare and elusive snow leopard.

The beautiful big cat was for Mathiessen a symbol of the mystery and ultimate reality that lies hidden barely beneath the surface of everyday life. The cat is seldom seen by those who have looked for it directly. It hides so well that observers have been known to stare at it from only a few feet away and yet not see it. Instead, the greatest number of sightings have been made by those studying the bharal, or blue sheep. Since the leopard feeds on these animals, it has most often been sighted in that tedious endeavor, indirectly, out of the corner of the eye.

Ultimate reality is distinct from our daily work, but it is seen in the process of doing it. God can be seen and encountered in drudgery and the tedious. That is because he who calls us to work daily is daily weaving what we do into what he is doing. We don't find meaning by running away from the mundane, we find meaning by vigorously applying ourselves to the mundane, in the name of Jesus Christ, and in the confidence that he is quietly and inexorably unfolding his purposes in history.

Find Your Place

The Great Drama we perform and celebrate in worship frames our daily work with meaning and mystery. It also places us in our work. Each human story finds meaning when it becomes part of the Great Story. Each of us has a role to play in the Drama of Salvation. Not to play that role is to miss our reason for living. The key to happiness is not to do our own thing, but to find our place in God's drama.

Joni Eareckson Tada sings a song that gives eloquent expression to what is perhaps the greatest frustration of my life. How much of what I am so busy doing is what God has called me to do? And how much of it is simply following the urges of my friends and culture? Most of the things I do are good things, but are they the best, are they what need to be done by me? What did God create me, Ben Patterson, to do?

> I play so many games,
> I have so many faces,
> I've run so many races that need not be run by me.
> I talk so many ways,
> I know so many stories,
> I sing so many ballads that need not be sung by me.
>
> O Lord, dear Lord, great author of the play,
> may I in wisdom learn the only part that I need play
> is the part that you wrote for me,
> the part that you wrote for me.

A friend of mine tells me he has a recurring nightmare. He is standing in the presence of God, at the end of his life, and God is shaking his head saying, "Clarence, you didn't do

what I made you to do, you didn't do what you are best at."
Nothing is worse than a wasted life. And a life is wasted if it is
not spent doing what the Writer of the play had in mind, even
if it made a huge income along the way. But life is filled with
meaning when we embrace the role God has written for us,
no matter how small, and play it to the hilt until the end.

We should choose our work in the light of our vocation:
what God has called each of us to in Christ. One good way
to figure out what that might be is on the basis of how our
God-given talents and gifts match up with what God wants
done in the world. Frederick Buechner's whimsical definition of vocation is just that: "The place God calls you to is
the place where your deep gladness and the world's deep
hunger meet."[7] That needs a lot more theological nuance to
cover all the facets of vocation, but it is a good rule of
thumb. And it highlights what is essential for us all: that our
work should be chosen and done in the light of God's Great
Story of Salvation.

A Symphony, Not a Rock Concert

The Great Story urges us to see our individual stories
and work as parts of a much larger thing that God is doing in
the world. The value of what we do is in relation to the larger
whole. Both worship and work are to be part of a symphony,
not a rock concert. In a rock concert, individual expression is
paramount; the individual performers use the group as a foil
to play off one another to enhance their own visibility.

In a symphony, individualism is sublimated for the sake
of the whole. The greater good of a community of performers
playing in concert more than makes up for the loss in individual expression. That's the biblical model.

This runs counter to the prevailing individualism of our
culture. The boom box is as apt a symbol for a rock culture
of individualistic self-assertion as can be found. I have seen
whole groups of people, supposedly together, standing with
these things on their shoulders, up against their ears, each

playing a different station or tape. With only a few changes, that is essentially the scene in the workplace today.

But the notion of work as an opportunity for individual- istic self-fulfillment is foreign to the Bible. If we work hard we do it for the sake of the Kingdom. If we get rich we do it for the sake of the Kingdom, never merely for our own sakes.

Apostasy is a strong biblical word used to describe those who have abandoned the faith. It consists of two Greek words, *apo*, meaning to leave, or abandon, and *stasis*, meaning place, or station. Its original usage was probably military; a soldier was apostate when he fled his post and abandoned it to the enemy. The Scriptures use it to describe those who have left the faith doctrinally, by heresy, or morally, by pagan lifestyle. I propose that our understanding of apostasy be expanded to include those who have abandoned the faith vocationally. The vocationally apostate man or woman sees his or her work only as an opportunity for individualistic self-fulfillment.

If we have learned anything from the moral and financial scandals that have plagued some television ministries in the past few years, it has been this: even so-called Christian min- istry can be pursued paganly, for the enhancement of in- dividuals, not for the good of the Kingdom. Opportunistic individualists have been out writing their own scripts, instead of finding where they fit in God's Story.

Vocational Training

The great Story we perform and celebrate in worship frames our lives, it places us in our work, and it trains us in carrying out our vocation. Our characters are trained and shaped and formed as we perform and practice the faith in the sanctuary week in and week out over a lifetime.

So powerful is the ritual drama of the Great Story that it moved a pastor to give an odd bit of advice to reluctant unbe- lievers—those who wished they could believe the gospel, but could not. He told them to go to worship each Sunday and sing and pray and listen, acting as though they believed it all to be true. He believed that the mere repetition of the words of worship, over a period of time, if spoken by a seeking heart, acting as if it believed them, would be used by the Holy Spirit to produce belief. I have one friend who was converted, following this advice.

The religion section of a newspaper reportedly printed a letter from a jaded churchgoer complaining that in a lifetime of church attendance, he calculated he had heard more than 5,000 sermons, and couldn't remember a single one. The letter touched off a heated debate in the mail about the value of sermons. One letter ended all the discussion. It said, "I have eaten well over 5,000 meals in my lifetime, and I can remember only a few of them. But I have the distinct feeling that without them I would have starved to death."

That is what the weekly performance of the Great Story, over a lifetime, does for the performance of our individual stories. It trains us in the living out of our vocations. On a single given Sunday, usually not a whole lot happens. But over a lifetime of Sundays, there is no calculating how much can happen.

When Life Whittles Us Down . . .

I have a theory about old age. It's very unscientific, but I hold it with deep conviction. I believe that when life has whittled us down, when joints have failed and skin has wrinkled and capillaries have clogged and hardened, what is left of us will be what we were all along, in our essence.

Exhibit A is a distant uncle. For the sake of my family, I'll call him Ray. All his life he did nothing but find new ways to get rich. A few of his schemes succeeded and he became a moderately wealthy man. He spent his senescence very comfortably, drooling and babbling constantly about the money he had made. I remember watching him when I was a child and even then being dumbstruck that he had wasted his whole life getting something which was so useless to him as he approached eternity. When life whittled him down to his essence, all there was left was raw greed. That was his ephemeral little story; that is what he had cultivated in a thousand little ways over a lifetime.

Exhibit B is my wife's grandmother. No need to protect family pride with her! Her name was Edna. When she died in her mid-eighties, she had already been senile for several years. What did this lady talk about? The best example I can think of was when we asked her to pray before dinner. She would reach out and hold the hands of those sitting beside her, a broad, beatific smile would spread across her face, her dim eyes would fill with tears as she looked up to heaven, and her chin would quaver as she poured out her love to Jesus. That was Edna in a nutshell. She loved Jesus and she loved people. She couldn't remember our names, but she couldn't keep her hands from patting us lovingly whenever we got near her.

When life whittled her down to her essence all there was left was love: love for God and love for people. That was her story! It too had been cultivated over years by a thousand little acts of worship and work. But it wasn't ephemeral, it was part of the Great Story. I am sure it is still being told at this moment.

9 ～

Never on Sunday

Once a friend of W. C. Fields walked into his dressing room and caught him reading the Bible. Knowing Fields's cynical attitude toward religion, he was surprised. Fields himself seemed embarrassed, quickly shut the book and explained why he was reading: "Just looking for loopholes," he said.

That little story captures some of the ambivalence I have felt most of my life toward the Sabbath, or the Lord's Day. I knew that it was special, and to be observed, but it seemed to me—especially as a child—to be so boring, dull, repressive and uninspiring. So I was always looking for loopholes: ways to get credit for observing it without really having to do so.

My best friend could play football on the Lord's Day, if he played quietly. The day was a mixed bag for me: I had to attend all the church services that day (bad), but I wasn't allowed to do homework (good). I couldn't go to the beach (bad), but my mother always prepared a big family dinner of roast beef and mashed potatoes and we all would fall asleep

111

on the floor afterward, watching the NFL game on television (good!).

I know many Christians who strive scrupulously to keep all the commandments but one: the Lord's Day. Like me, they are looking for loopholes. They know it is special, and to be observed, but they don't really know why or how. Frankly, attending religious services comes out a poor and distant second to all the other things one can do with a weekend, like going fishing, playing golf, or just sleeping in and enjoying the Sunday paper over several cups of coffee. Or, the Sabbath looms up as a barrier to getting some work done that must be done, whether piled up in the office from the week before or waiting in the yard from the month before.

So they always seem to be looking for loopholes: ways to get credit for keeping the Sabbath, without actually having to *keep* the Sabbath. Some play the percentages loophole: "Well, two out of four Sundays isn't too bad. In baseball, that would make me a 500 hitter." Others attempt the "have-your-cake-and-eat-it-too" loophole: they attend worship services, and then proceed to cram as much activity into the rest of the day as possible. The earlier the service, the better, for these folks. The more theologically sophisticated go for the "you-deserve-a-break-today" loophole. They stay away from church, explaining, "I've had a tough week. I'm exhausted. This is the one day I have to rest up or do some things around the house that just have to be done. Didn't Jesus say that the 'Sabbath was made for man, not man for the Sabbath'?"

Indeed, Jesus did say that it was for our sakes God gave the command to observe the Sabbath and to keep it holy (Mark 2:27). But that's the point, isn't it? In the Sabbath command God has said to us, "Here it is, I give it to you for your own health and happiness. Keep it and you win; violate it and you lose." If something is given for our sakes, and we refuse to receive it, then we hurt ourselves.

The Pharisees, to whom Jesus directed that famous statement, were violating the Sabbath. They were piling up so many rules defining how one should keep the day holy that the significance of the day was lost under the pile. But they violate it no more than we do when we commit the equal and opposite error and set no rules at all. They are guilty of the legalist sin, we of the antinomian sin. We both violate the Sabbath, and in the process hurt ourselves, the violators.

What do we miss when we lose the Sabbath? Or stated more positively, what do we gain when we observe the Sabbath as God intended it to be observed? We gain grace, freedom, hope and time.

Grace

One of the more than seven specifically teaching references to the Sabbath in the Bible is found in Exodus 20:8–11. There the meaning of the Sabbath is linked to God's work of creation:

> Remember the Sabbath day by keeping it holy. Six days you shall labor and do all your work, but the seventh day is a Sabbath to the Lord your God. On it you shall not do any work, neither you, nor your son or daughter, nor your manservant or maidservant, nor your animals, nor the alien within your gates. *For in six days the Lord made the heavens and the earth, the sea, and all that is in them, but he rested on the seventh day. Therefore the Lord blessed the Sabbath day and made it holy* (emphasis mine).

This text tells us that built into the creation, from the very beginning, was rest. That is literally what the word Sabbath means: to rest, to cease, to pause. This rest tells us that there is a rhythm and a pattern built into the structure of the world. The rhythm is that God has created us to need an alternation in our lives between work and rest. Without it our lives go sour. During the aftermath of the French Revolution, the Sabbath was abolished, being substituted with one day of rest in ten. Voltaire was quoted as saying, "We cannot destroy Christianity until we first destroy the Christian Sabbath."[1] But the experiment was a disaster: men and

women crumbled under the strain and animals literally col
lapsed in the streets.

A Pattern of Grace

There is also a pattern to this rhythm: it moves not out of
work to rest, but out of rest to work. The biblical reckoning of
the day is not as we reckon it, from sunup to sunup, but from
sundown to sundown. Throughout the story of creation in
Genesis 1 is a litany, measuring each day of creation with
these words:

> *And there was evening, and there was morning—the first
> day* . . . .
> *And there was evening, and there was morning—the second
> day* . . . .
> *And there was evening, and there was morning—the third
> day* . . . . (the fourth day, the fifth day, etc.)

Each new day begins not with people getting up to work,
but with people lying down to rest! So the Jewish Sabbath
begins not on Saturday morning, but on Friday evening. The
pleasure of this pattern is easily verifiable. Compare how you
feel on your day off if you begin it in the evening before the
day with how you feel if you begin it the morning of the day.
If you had to work the evening before, you awake the next
morning tired, don't you? You don't feel really rested and
refreshed until noon and the day is half over. But if you begin
it the evening before, you awake the next morning already
refreshed and ready to enjoy the whole day.

The implications for work are revolutionary. When I
wake up in the morning, my tendency is to get out of bed, hit
the floor running and rush out the front door, knot in stom-
ach, coffee in hand. I'm thinking, *I've got to go out there and
make something happen.* But something has already been
happening: God has been at work while I slept. My job is not
to go out and make something happen, but to discover where
I fit in with what God has already been doing.

That is why it is so important to begin the day with prayer. It is presumptuous to begin any other way! As workers, it is our first responsibility to check in with the boss and get in tune with what he has been doing while we slept and what he requires of us while we are awake. To just get up and rush into the day is to presume that we are the ones who are in charge of our lives and our work.

The order, or pattern of creation, is the same as the order or pattern of salvation: In all things we are to move not from work to grace, but from grace to work—otherwise grace is not grace, but wages! Paul's great words in Ephesians 2:8–10 capture this pattern neatly: "It is by grace you have been saved, through faith—and this is not from yourselves, it is the gift of God—not by works, so that no one can boast. For we are God's workmanship, created in Christ Jesus to do good works. . . ."

There is the pattern: God saves us because of his grace; salvation is his gift, not his reward for good work, *it is the gift of God—not by works.* But he gives us his grace that we might work—*For we are God's workmanship, created in Christ Jesus to do good works.* As with salvation, so with the creation: we don't work to receive grace, we receive grace to work.

The first message of the Sabbath to us, then, is grace. The Sabbath is a day of grace. It says to us that God is God and we are only people, and that is good. We can leave the running of the universe to him. All we need do is find our place in his scheme. Work, this side of the Fall, has a way of pressing us all down and burying us under its weight. But the Sabbath, even this side of the Fall, is a word of grace spoken into the lives of driven, harassed workers. It says to housewives and account executives, to welders and attorneys, "You may stop now—no, you must stop now—at least for a day." Even to non-Christians it says, "Your life is not all law and necessity. The Lord of creation who causes his sun to shine on both the good and the evil, has also given you this grace and this freedom from work."

When the Bible links the Sabbath to the creation, it is telling us that there is a rhythm and a pattern of grace built into us by God that cannot be violated with impunity.

Freedom

The Bible also links the Sabbath to freedom. Deuteronomy 5:15 gives a theological rationale for the day that is different from the one found in Exodus 20. It mandates the observance of the day and then gives this explanation for why: "Remember that you were slaves in Egypt and that the Lord your God brought you out of there with an outstretched arm. Therefore the Lord has commanded you to observe the Sabbath day."

God is saying, "Once you were slaves and had to work or die. Now you are free. Don't ever forget it. Lest you do forget it, be sure to observe the Sabbath. Stop working once a week to remember that you are free, not slaves."

The Sabbath is therefore a freedom day in a world that lives under the slavery of work. It's a world that says you must justify your existence and sustain yourself by achievement. Our speech abounds with sayings that point to this reality: "If you think nobody cares if you're alive, try missing a few car payments," or, "If you haven't got an ulcer, you're not carrying your share of the load" are but a few.

The cartoon "Sally Forth" had its heroine Sally making out her list of things "to do" one morning. She was thinking as she wrote, "At the start of the week, this woman makes out a list of things to do. It serves to remind her of what she needs to accomplish. It also serves to remind her that the waves are lapping at her chin, and she's about to drown in a sea of work."

Frantic Recreation

Even our recreation and leisure have the marks of slavery on them. For my Dad's generation, Sunday was the day to rest up from the week before and for the week to come. For my generation, Sunday is the day to reward yourself for all the stuff you put up with the week before. There is a frantic, deadly seriousness to recreation these days. It has almost a moral "oughtness" to it. People feel that they "owe" it to themselves to play on Saturday and Sunday. Both generations are slaves to work because for both it is work that defines the meaning of rest.

The beauty of the command to keep the Sabbath holy is that it empowers us to deflate all the imperial claims that work would make on our lives. It enables us to look it in the eye and say, "No! I am not your slave! I'm stopping for the next twenty-four hours. In Christ I am free. My future well-being is in his hands, not in how well my hands serve you."

The beauty of this statement is that it is a command. We would rarely rest if we were given the choice. We need to be ordered by the Almighty to rest, or else we'll keep on obeying the orders of almighty work. There can be a great delight in looking at a pile of work and saying, on the Sabbath, "No, not today, you'll just have to wait until tomorrow," no matter what "has to happen" the next day.

This doesn't mean that we don't do things which truly must be done on the Sabbath. Jesus noted that if an ox fell into a ditch on the Sabbath, the Law made provision for it to be pulled out. Sometimes things just must be done on that day. But Billy Graham commented: "If your ox keeps falling in a ditch on the Sabbath, you'd better fill in the ditch or tie up the ox." We need to so order our lives that we can stop at least one day a week without causing everything we're doing to come crashing down around us.

Hope

The Sabbath is also about hope. Hope is implicit in the Genesis story of creation, and in the structure of the week. There is a movement from the beginning to the end. There is not the endless repetition of cycles, but culmination, resolution, completion, consummation. For Judaism the week became a picture of history, of life lived toward the consummation, the end of all things and God's denouement of the human drama. It also became the centerpiece of the week. For three days before the Sabbath, the devout Jew looked forward to it. Then, for three days afterward he looked back and savored what it had been. God's eternal rest was the hope the Jew looked for and out of which he lived.

For the Christian church, the Sabbath was moved to Sunday because it was the day of the week on which Jesus was raised from the dead. In Christ the new life hoped for in Judaism was inaugurated by the resurrection. Now what had been lived *toward* was to be lived *from,* even though it was yet to be fully accomplished.

The hope theme is explicit in the message of the Book of Hebrews, in the New Testament: "There remains, then, a Sabbath-rest for the people of God; for anyone who enters God's rest also rests from his own work, just as God did from his. Let us, therefore, make every effort to enter that rest . . ."(4:9–11a).

A Window to the Future

The Sabbath is therefore a window to the future. It points to the time when God will make sense of this mess. It tells us that there is more than just the inexorable march of time. It reminds us that there is meaning to our lives beyond the rat race.

Poet George Herbert wrote of the Sabbath:

> O day most calm, most bright,
> The fruit of this, the next world's bud.[2]

If it is true that a day of rest in this world is the "bud" of the world to come, then I can truly rest in hope the rest of the week! If rest is the "bud" of the future, then the future is not in my hands, but in God's. This hope saves me from the hubris that gives idolatrous significance to the work I do through the week. If the Lord doesn't build the house, then whatever I do is done in vain. The future is in his hands, not mine.

But this hope also saves me from the despair that says nothing I do matters. Since the future is in his hands, he can take what I do and make it matter as he both weaves it into his grand scheme of redemption and gives me my daily bread, to boot.

Take this hope out of work and joy quickly disappears too. The work we do becomes a meaningless drudgery. As apt an image of our times as I have ever read is found in C. S. Lewis's children's story, *The Silver Chair*. When the children Jill and Eustace enter the underground world of the witch, they discover there is no sun shining there, only dim, pale light revealing thousands of silent gnomes with blank faces, working: "Every gnome seemed to be as busy as it was sad, though Jill never found out what they were so busy about. But the endless moving, shoving, hurrying and the soft pad, pad, pad [of their feet] went on."[3]

Could that "soft pad, pad, pad" be also the steady drone of automobile engines on our freeways taking dazed men and women to work? The meaning is gone because what they do is done without hope.

Rest or Therapy?

Christopher Lasch wrote his *Culture of Narcissism* in an attempt to understand what happens when a society, such as ours, begins to lose its confidence in the future. He concluded that people " . . . hunger not for personal salvation, but for the feeling, the momentary illusion, of personal well-being, health and psychic security."[4]

They seek therapy, not redemption; diversion, not rest; a holiday, not the grace, freedom and hope of the Sabbath.

I read of a Soviet furniture factory in which frustrated, bored workers can book ten minutes in a "Psychological Relief Room." It reportedly has upholstered rocking chairs,

recorded bird calls playing in the background, scenic photo-
graphs projected on the walls, and a female voice singing to
a Latin beat:

> Have a happy rest.
> This day is very happy.
> We shouldn't be sad.
> It will always be like this.
> There will always be Summer.[5]

That's not rest, it's therapy. But therapy is the closest a
Sabbath-less and hope-less world gets to rest.

Time

In the Sabbath we also gain time. What Jesus said about
losing our lives to find them (Mark 8:35) is true also of time.
Remarkably, it is the time we give to God on this day that we
get back.

The logic of this starts with the basic truth that just as
God is Lord of all creation, he is also Lord of time. He controls
time, using the sun, moon and stars he created to mark off
"seasons and days and years" (Gen. 1:14). He fills time with
what he ordains, giving a time for everything he desires, a
"season for every activity under heaven," including the time
for our birth and death. Every moment and every element of
our lives comes from the all-wise and all-loving hand of the
God who is Lord of time (Eccl. 3:1–7).

The Sanctification of Time

The Sabbath is an emphatic reminder that God is the
Lord of time. Over and over again, the Bible gives the Sabbath the title, "the Lord's Holy Day." Holy means set apart
for God, sanctified or consecrated to him; a day is a unit of
time. "The Lord's Holy Day" speaks of time sanctified and
consecrated to God. To be sure, all our days are the Lord's
not just the Sabbath. But the idea of the Sabbath is to sanctify

a part for the sake of the whole. Just as Christians are the salt of the earth, so the Sabbath is the salt of the week and of time. We observe the Lord's Day not because only this day is the Lord's, but because all days are the Lord's, and the Sabbath reminds us of that radical truth.

Here we come upon the great contrast between pagan religion and the religion of the Bible. Pagan religion concerned itself with the consecration of space. Above all, it was places that were holy—nations and mountains, temples and groves. In Canaanite religion, the faith of the peoples that surrounded Israel, the gods or Baals were gods of the earth and of agriculture.

But Judaism, with its strong biblical roots, was "a religion of time aimed at the sanctification of time," writes Jewish Theologian Abraham Heschel.[6] There was a temple and there was Jerusalem and there was the land God gave Israel, and these were holy to God. But before any of these, and after all of these disappeared, there were the great days to celebrate God's love and salvation. If the temples of paganism were holy architecture in space, the Jewish holy days and feasts were holy "architecture in time," with the Sabbath the chief structure: the "palace" or "cathedral" in time.[7]

According to Heschel, modern technical civilization is essentially pagan in its preoccupation with the conquest and manipulation of space—of things and objects. Moreover, technical civilization seems always to gain space at the expense of time. The more we have of things, it seems the less we have of time. I am writing this book on a word processor that has cut by 40 percent the amount of time it takes me to write anything. Has it saved me any time? Not really. Now that I have this new-fangled thing which makes me able to write so much more so much faster, I am now writing twice as much as I used to. The net result is that I am even busier now than I was when all I had was a pen and a notebook!

But time, not space and things, is at the heart of our existence, says Heschel.[8] Technical civilization looks for meaning in things; the faith of the Bible looks for meaning in time, for it was "when the *time* had fully come" that God brought us salvation in his Son (Gal. 4:4, emphasis mine).

Chronos or Kairos?

The Bible's interest in the sanctification of time is best seen from the perspective of two Greek words for time. One of these is virtually absent from the Bible, the other is the almost exclusive biblical word for time. The first is the word *chronos*. It means time as seen from a quantitative, linear perspective. The second word is *kairos*, meaning time seen from the perspective of its quality and meaning. To contrast the two, *chronos* means time as an abstract dimension, *kairos* means time as concrete circumstances; *chronos* is a date, *kairos* is a season; *chronos* is something to manage and control, *kairos* is something to understand and obey.

Which word do you think is the one used almost exclusively in the Bible to refer to time? If you guessed *kairos*, you would be correct. The Bible seems to be almost completely uninterested in time as *chronos*, and totally fascinated with time as *kairos*. It is far more interested in the meaning of the time given to us than it is in the amount of time we have.

It's not hard to see which view of time prevails in our culture. We are a people obsessed with *chronos*, how to get more of it, how to control it and manage it. Some social analysts believe the invention of the clock has had a more radical effect on the shape human civilization has taken than any other event in the past 500 years. Certainly our lives have been conditioned by the social experience of the wristwatch.

How silly this all looks when time is seen from the perspective of the Bible, as *kairos*. We are very concerned about the management of time, aren't we? Time management treats time as a substance to consume, not events to respond to. Time management! The notion is preposterous! Worse than that, it is presumptuous. Who could presume to manage *kairos*? What we really do with all this time management technique is to find ways to do more things within the time we have been given: more people to see, more meetings to attend, more books to write. This is why we still feel empty and spent when we have done all that managing. We assume we need help to manage time because we are too busy. The deeper issue is that we are too busy because we have lost a sense of the meaning of time.

The Bible calls us to live first by kairos, and to let *kairos* dictate to *chronos* what we will do and how we will live. Paul uses the word *kairos* when he reminds the Christians in Rome to understand "the present time." He is urging them to be alert to the season, to the meaning of the moment in the light of Christ's resurrection and return. To discern the *kairos* will mean to "behave decently, as in the daytime" (Rom. 13:11, 13). The Greek word translated "decently" in the NIV is *euschemon,* a word that carries with it the ideas of elegance and grace. To really know the time is to live gracefully and elegantly, with class, if you will. It is to live as befits the season.

Do You Really Know What Time It Is?

The morning after my engagement to my wife, I was caught in a traffic jam with thousands of other men and women trying to get to work before their wristwatches said 8:00 A.M. The year was 1970 and my car radio was playing a popular song by the rock group *Chicago.* It talked about people rushing through a park on their way to work, wearing gold watches as the singer asked, "Does anybody really know what time it is?" The song was unwittingly about *kairos* and how it is so easily lost in *chronos.* That morning was one of the happiest of my life: the night before I had heard the girl of my dreams tell me she would be my wife. I wanted to stop my yellow Volkswagen right in the middle of the freeway, stand on its roof and shout to the people around me locked in their cars, "Does anybody really know what time it is?"

We need the Sabbath to remind us what time it really is: the time between the resurrection of Jesus and his return to earth. We need the Sabbath to interrupt our *chronos* and point to the meaning of time so we can live and work with elegance and class. We need the Sabbath to remind us that, since God is Lord of time, we live by grace, not work; freedom, not slavery; and hope, not despair.

God interrupted my *chronos* with a Sabbath of sorts back in 1979, when I ruptured a disc in my lower back and was forced to endure complete bed rest, flat on my back, for six weeks. It was a maddening time: there was absolutely nothing I could do to get anything done. Even the massive amounts of reading I hoped to get done while convalescing was short-circuited by the fact that my eyes wouldn't focus well while I was lying on my back.

About all I could do was pray. Since I am a pastor, I thought I might get something done for the church by praying for the entire membership each day. So I did, going through the whole directory daily, praying for each church member by name. At first it was little more than just something to relieve the boredom, but after a while it became sweet. Near the time I was to be able to go back to work, I found myself saying to the Lord one day, "It's too bad I don't have time to pray this way when I am well."

God's response was quick and blunt. He said, "You have the same amount of time when you are well as when you are sick. The only difference is that when you are well you think *you* are in control of things." In other words, I, you, we all have the same amount of *chronos* each day: twenty-four hours, no more, no less. What we lack is a sense of *kairos*, the discernment to see what the time means and what God requires of us in it. That Sabbath, as will all Sabbaths, had a beautiful way of sensitizing me to *kairos* and thus regaining for me the time of which I never seem to have enough.

By now I hope we can see why Jesus said to the Pharisees—who were abusing the day in the opposite way that we abuse it: "The Sabbath was made for man, not man for the Sabbath." It is for us. It is a gift. As with all God's laws, it is about grace and freedom and hope. If it comes to us as an order, it is only because we need to be commanded to stop our work. If it were only a permission, few of us would stop, we are so anxious about our work and our recreation. But beneath the command is a permission: a permission to relax in the grace of God and be free in his love and encouraged by his hope.

Question: Is there anything about your week that says loud and clear that God is the center out of which everything flows and around which everything is to find its place? Henry Zylstra asked how a man from Mars might perceive the role religion plays in American life: "He could . . . . take a copy of *Time* magazine, point to its table of contents, and say that what he had found down here was a lot of people interested in Art, Books, Business, Cinema, Education, Medicine, Music, People, Personality, Press, Radio, Religion, Sports, Theatre . . . ."[9]

Religion is just one of the many things we do, no better, no worse than the rest. When I look at the frantic pace of our lives, when I see how full we cram our days with activities, most of them good, I question our concept of time. When I see how much the Sabbath is just another way of doing what we do the rest of the week, I wonder if it is even possible for us to really believe and know that Christ is Lord of all, the beginning and the end, the One in whom we live and move and have our being.

The Sabbath says, "Stop. Look. Listen. Life is passing you by. The harder you run, the more behind you get; the fuller you try to be, the more empty you become." Stop. Look. Listen. Celebrate the Sabbath. Know that you live by grace, not by work. Know that you are free. You are not a slave to "necessity." Know that there is hope, that your life is moving to a grand consummation, and that it will get there by God's doing, not your own. Stop. Look. Listen.

> Have your heart right with Christ, and He
> will visit you often, and so turn weekdays
> into Sundays, meals into sacraments, homes
> into temples and earth into heaven.
>
> *Charles Haddon Spurgeon*

10 ~

Our Daily Bread

"The Lord Jesus Christ requests the pleasure of your company at a banquet to be held in his honor." Those were the words I read on an invitation to celebrate Communion. I liked that. I was being invited to have dinner with some friends at a banquet held in Christ's honor . . . . And much, much more.

The much more has to do with our work. Holy Communion is the covergent point where all the Bible has to say about work and worship comes together and is embodied in bread and wine. No other act of worship has more power to inform and transform our work than this simple and mysterious meal. If God can be real to you at the Lord's Table, then he will be real to you at your desk or workbench.

A Special Kind of Remembrance

How? The remembrance of Communion is the key-stone of its significance for our work. On the night he was betrayed, Jesus broke bread and said these familiar words, as reported by Paul, "'This is my body, which is for you; do this in *remembrance* of me.' In the same way, after supper he took the cup, saying, 'This cup is the new covenant in my blood; do this, whenever you drink it, in *remembrance* of me'" (1 Cor. 11:25, italics mine).

Anamnesis is the Greek word we translate "remembrance" in most English versions of the New Testament. It expresses a Hebrew and Semitic concept with no real parallel in English. None of our words really capture what it means. Words like remembrance, commemoration, memorial—these all carry with them the idea that the thing or person remembered is past and gone. They suggest images of musing through a photo album and remembering the old days. *Anamnesis* suggests just the opposite. According to the *Westminster Dictionary of Worship,* when we remember, in the sense of *anamnesis,* the person or the thing in the past, it is brought into the present. In *anamnesis,* what or who *was* is made *now.* [1]

The early church understood the remembrance of Communion in this sense. Communion was not an instructive object lesson in something that once happened. It was the "re-calling" before God of all that Christ did for us in his death and resurrection. But re-call was not mere recollection. It was re-call in the sense of calling forth once again what had been. It was the body and blood of Christ that heals our brokenness and nurtures our faith.

In the remembrance, or *anamnesis,* of Communion, more happens than mere memory. Jesus himself is present and experienced in a special way. We meet *him* in the bread and cup.

They're Both the Same Daddy!

A young couple had their first child, a girl, when the father was stationed overseas during the World War Two. For the first two years of her life, all the child saw of her father was a photograph her mother had framed and set on the kitchen table. Her mother taught her to say "daddy" whenever she saw it.

Finally her daddy came home. The whole family waited breathlessly to see the delight in the little girl's face when she, at long last, saw her daddy. But when she saw him she cried and ran away. She wouldn't come near this stranger. Instead, she would run to the picture, point at the man there, stamp her foot and insist, "That's my daddy!" Her mom and dad were heartbroken.

Then one day as she sat at the kitchen table eating breakfast, she looked long and hard at the stranger sitting with her and then long and hard at the daddy in the picture. Her eyes went back to the stranger and then back to the picture. Then her face lit up and she exclaimed, "They're both the same daddy!"

Mystery

The Christ we meet by faith in the bread and cup, and the Christ who died and was raised for our sakes, is the same Christ. Just how and in what way he meets us has been the subject of endless and tiresome debate. It has generated a whole vocabulary of disputation: words and phrases like transubstantiation, consubstantiation, real presence and the like. This must break the heart of God. Communion and Baptism, the two great sacramental signs of Christian unity, have become battlegrounds. What was meant to unite us has divided us.

Communion is a mystery to wonder at, not an idea to argue over. I think Jesus would say to the centuries of theological squabbles in the church over the meaning of Communion, "Look, it's a mystery! Why can't you learn to live with that? Just shut up and eat—and be filled with wonder."

The mystery of the *anamnesis* of Communion is that God somehow meets us in the common elements of bread and wine. That, in turn, points to a broader mystery. Bread and wine are products of creation. Not only that, they are also the work of human hands. Farmers, bakers, drivers, vintners, merchants— a whole community of labor is represented in the bread and the cup. The broader mystery is that God chooses to meet us through his creation and through the work we do. The mystery of Christ's presence in Communion is not different in *kind* from the mystery of his presence in the world and in our work. The only difference is in *degree.* The presence of God that we see and experience in Communion is a sharper focus, a greater concentration, of the mystery of his presence in the world he created—and in the work he has commanded us to do in his world.

Holy Communion says that if the true and living God can be met at the Lord's Table, then he can also be met at the shop where the table was made. It says that if we can encounter him in the bread and wine, then we can also encounter him where those elements were grown and manufactured and sold. We can even meet him on the highways that transported them from field to market to sanctuary. Holy Communion says God can be met wherever we earn our daily bread.

One Huge Reality

If we are alienated from our work it may be because we are first alienated from the material creation in which we do that work. One of the blind spots of our age is that we have a tendency to grossly underestimate the significance of the physical world God made. We miss what it means to say *God* created the world. But if he made it, it must be good. Very good. In the creation story in Genesis 1, that is what God says over and over again: "It is good!" He says it of dolphins and kelp, jacaranda trees and rose bushes, Orion and Andromeda, cows and beavers. He says it of apricots and bananas, canyons and coastlines. He says it of people, especially people.

This world is good because it was made by a good God. God says it is so good that it is a worthy vehicle to show something of his character and majesty. "O Lord, our Lord, how majestic is your name in all the earth!" says Psalm 8. The heavens preach about him. Says Psalm 19, they "declare the glory of God."

Not only is the world good, but there is much more to it than meets the eye. Biblical cosmology includes both the seen and the unseen, the visible and the invisible. It is an unbiblical dualism to speak of the physical as one reality and the spiritual as another. God made it all and it is all together one huge reality. We live in one reality, part of which our physical senses are equipped to see, part of which they are not.

Reductionism and Escapism

As a culture we bounce back and forth between the extremes of a reductionistic naturalism on the one hand, and an escapist mysticism on the other. The reductionists tell us this physical world is all there is and that it is physical through and through, no more and no less. What you see and touch and measure, they insist, is what you get—all you get. When it comes to having any meaning or mystery or relation to a larger reality, their cosmos is as flat and one-dimensional as people once believed the world to be before the time of Columbus.

I will never forget a conversation over dinner one night with a friend who had graduated from Cal Tech with a Master's degree in engineering. I was holding forth on the beauties of what I consider to be the greatest natural wonder I have ever laid eyes on, the Grand Canyon. He listened to me as I practically babbled about the mysterium tremendum of its sheer size and the delicate beauty of its colors. They change from moment to moment as the sun moves across the sky above it. I spoke with enthusiasm and wonder.

Then he said to me ruefully, "That's what you see when you look at the Canyon with your overheated religious imagination. All I can see when I look into it is millennia of water and ice and wind carving that hole into the shape it is today. To me it is a mechanical marvel, not a mystery."

It is a poor person indeed who can look at the Grand Canyon and see only the action of water and ice and wind over millennia. The Grand Canyon is more than the sum total of its parts. So is everything else in creation. "We are a faint tracing on the surface of mystery," writes Annie Dillard. Those who would reduce this universe to nothing more than the sum of its component parts are afflicted with what she describes as "the cocksure air of a squatter who has come to feel he owns the place."[2]

Someone has said that philosophy begins with the question of why there is something here as opposed to there—not being something here. Why this world and this universe? Why these planets and stars instead of nothing at all? The brute fact that all of this is here and that we are here and we know it, defies analysis. It strains the imagination to the breaking point and renders anyone with eyes to see it, mute before the mystery. The reductionist suffers from a case of existential myopia.

On the other hand there is the kind of mystic who would seek somehow to escape this vulgar and constricting physical world of flesh, blood and gravity. He or she would sail away into the freedom of pure thought, spirit and ecstasy. Some Christians confuse this world-denying escapism with what the Bible teaches about heaven and the life beyond the grave. But the Bible teaches that our hope lies not in immortal souls living forever in a disembodied eternity in the skies, but in the resurrection: new and transformed bodies living in a new and transformed heaven and earth. In other words, God likes this material stuff he made so much that he plans not to destroy it, but to raise it up one day, new and glorified.

Incarnation

The Incarnation is decisive in this biblical cosmology. Jesus was the God/man. Heaven and earth, the seen and the unseen, came together in perfect harmony in him. In Christ, flesh and blood were fit vehicles to mediate the very presence of God himself. But the Incarnation could not have taken place unless the creation, the material world, was good and a part of a still larger reality that we cannot see. The Incarnation is of "one good fabric" with the whole creation, seen and unseen. The Word which spoke this "one huge world" into existence is the same Word which met us in the physical body of Jesus of Nazareth, first century Palestinian Jew.

The Incarnation is the paradigm through which we must understand the world, our work, the sacraments—and their relation to each other. The Incarnation is the model of the unity and wholeness of life as God created it to be. It is God's decisive statement to us that the world he made is good, despite the invasion of sin; and that it remains the place where God chooses to have communion with us. The Incarnation shows how the sacred can suffuse the common, how the spiritual animates the physical.

Not a Sacrament, but Sacramental

Augustine defined a sacrament as a visible sign of an invisible reality. By this definition Christ, God incarnate, is the supreme sacrament. There was much, much more to him than what met the eye. When you saw him you saw a first-century Palestinian Jew. When you touched him you touched real flesh. But there was much more—there before you was also the Word of God, the eternal Son of the Father, the second Person of the Trinity.

In this same sense, but to a lesser degree, the whole world is sacramental. Because the visible and the invisible are part of one huge, mysterious world, we can know there is always much more to the world we see than meets the eye. By the grace of God, through faith, the material world is capable of conveying the presence of the God who made it.

The creation. The Incarnation. The sacraments. The God who met us supremely and uniquely in the physical body of Jesus meets us also in his world and through his sacraments. The bread and cup we use in Communion are of the same good fabric as the creation and the Incarnation. As with the Incarnation, this sacrament is possible because of a creation that is itself sacramental.

Visible Signs of Invisible Reality

Welch's grape juice. DiCarlo's French bread. Those are the brands our church uses in Communion. We get them at a local supermarket. There's nothing impressive about them. We use one to stand for the body of Christ, the other to symbolize his blood. But when offered to God and blessed, when received in faith, by God's mercy they become more than the sum of their parts. They become visible signs of an invisible reality. In a unique way, they become the physical means by which we experience the grace of God.

Housewife. Short order cook. Stockbroker. There's nothing very impressive about any of these, either. Most jobs, even the most glamorous, have a way of becoming depressingly common and, well, daily. But the message of the mystery of the bread and cup of Communion is that they all have the possibility of becoming, if not sacraments, sacramental. Because they are part of a creation that is itself sacramental they all can become visible signs of an invisible reality—unless, of course they are dishonest or destructive. When a job is offered to God in faith, he blesses it and it becomes a means not only of serving him in his world, but of encountering him there.

Offering

The offering of our work to God is crucial. Our word *sacrament* comes from a Latin word, *sacramentum*. A *sacramentum* was the oath or pledge of absolute loyalty that a Roman soldier made to his general. It is not difficult to see how appropriate this word is for Communion. Communion is a remembrance, or *anamnesis*, of Christ's *sacramentum*, his pledge of love and grace to us on the cross. In the broken

bread and poured-out cup, Jesus symbolically offers himself
to us in love. He gives us his oath, his pledge!

But it works also from the other direction. In Communion we symbolically give Christ our oath of love and devotion,
our *sacramentum*, too. That is the chief reason another of the
words for Communion is Eucharist. Eucharist is a Greek word
that means "thanksgiving." Isaac Watts's great gospel hymn,
"When I Survey," says it well: "Love so amazing, so divine/
Demands my soul, my life, my all." Paraphrased in the terms
of Communion, such a great *sacramentum* demands my *sacramentum*; such a great oath of love *to* me demands an equally
great oath of love *from* me! Gratitude can do no less.

One of the most memorable Communions in which I
ever shared climaxed with the pastor praying, "So, Lord, may
we too be broken bread and poured-out wine for you." I had
never thought of it that way before. The bread and the cup of
Communion, and the events they point to, were meant also to
externalize the dispositions of our hearts. We should look at
the broken bread and poured-out cup and say, "That's me,
too, Lord—for you!"

I saw a Ziggy cartoon in which the droll little character
was walking by a church marquee displaying the title of that
Sunday's sermon. It was, "Come In and Altar Your Life." That
is what Christian worship is all about—the "altaring" of our
lives. It is the placing of our lives on the altar, the offering of
our bodies as "living sacrifices," to use the words of St. Paul.

A word of caution is in order. We do not present ourselves because we are worthy to make an acceptable offering
to God. The only acceptable oblation that could ever be made
is the offering of the body of his Holy Son, Jesus Christ.
But since we are, by faith, incorporated into his Body, the
Church, we can offer ourselves as members of his Body. Re-
ferring to Communion, Augustine said that Jesus is both the
priest who offers the sacrifice, and the sacrifice itself. But
included in his offering is his Body, the Church.[3]

It was the practice of the early church to take the offering just prior to celebrating Communion. The people would

walk to the Lord's Table and place upon it food they had prepared at home to be eaten in the meal. It was food they had grown in their own gardens or had bought in the market. As Alan Richardson points out in his book, *The Biblical Doctrine of Work*, the food that was offered was *the product of human labor.* [4] These products were offered to God in gratitude (Eucharist!) for his sacrifice on the cross and then blessed and served as the symbols of the Body and Blood of Christ. In other words, the offering of the people became the symbols of the sacrifice of Christ in the sacrament of Communion. The offering they made was not only a token of their very lives, but of the work of human hands.

It is so easy for us to miss this today in the way we celebrate Communion. The offering we make is so antiseptic and feels so removed from the work we do. We reach into our pockets, pull out our wallets, and put some money in a plate as we talk to our neighbor about what we're going to do after church. In most evangelical churches, the offering is only marginally related to Communion in the minds of the people. In many it is seen as a fund-raising activity, a necessary evil intruding itself into the sanctity of worship. Not so! The offering is integral to Christian worship. It is the symbol of what we are to do with our lives and our work. The offering should be the sign, par excellence, of our *sacramentum* to Christ in the work we do through the week. We should see the elements on the Lord's Table as signs, not only of his Body and Blood, but of ourselves and our work.

Sanctity

"To sacrifice something," writes Frederick Buechner, "is to make it holy by giving it away for love." [5] The great mystery and meaning of Communion for our work is this: the offering we make of ourselves and our work is sanctified, or made holy, when it is offered in love. It then comes back to us as sacrament. We bring our gifts to the Lord's Table, signified by the Bread and Cup. These things—things that we give—

are blessed and then given back to us to eat and drink as the symbols of the very Body and Blood of Christ! Because of Christ's first great *sacramentum,* we make our *sacramentum* to him. Then, the very things we have given away come back as sacraments: means, vehicles of grace and communion with our Lord. In short, our lives and our work are sanctified. Mystery!

There is a lovely picture of this in the sixth chapter of John's Gospel. Jesus and his disciples are confronted with 5,000 people who need to be fed. There isn't enough food to feed them all. But a boy brings five barley loaves and two fishes, the fruits of someone's labor, and offers them to Jesus. Then, in the language of Communion, John tells us that the Lord "took the loaves, gave thanks, and distributed to those who were seated," and 5,000 people were fed. Before the Lord's Supper was instituted, Jesus was already sanctifying lives and work offered to him in faith. He was using them as means of his grace and love, making them his *sacramentum.*

George Herbert, the great seventeenth century priest and poet of vocation, prayed that God would teach him to see God in all the work he did and enable him to do all his work as unto God. This, he said, was the thing that would make ordinary work extraordinary. For it would not only make all his work a *service* to God, it would also make his work *communion* with God! Then God would graciously touch his humble work and make it his own.

> A servant with this clause
> Makes drudgerie divine;
> Who sweeps a room as for Thy laws
> Makes that and the action fine . . . .
> For that which God doth touch and own
> Cannot for lesse be told.[6]

Tubes, Bootstraps and Synergy

In his fine book, *The Physical Side of Being Spiritual,* Peter Gillquist writes of the two errors into which we fall regarding our work. They are equal and opposite. The first is what he calls "Tube Theology." This is the notion that humans are merely conduits through which God wants to do his work. The goal of this theology is to so let go of our own initiative and will that the Holy Spirit can take us over completely and we no longer live and work for God, but he lives and works through us. This is the passive error about work. The other error is its opposite: "Bootstrap Theology." It says, "God has given you everything you need to do what he wants you to do, so just get out there and do it." This is the active error.[7]

The biblical position is what Gillquist calls "Synergy." The word synergy is derived from two Greek words, *syn*, "the same as," or "together with," and *ergos*, which means "work" or "energy." This is the view of work espoused by the apostle Paul when he described himself and his colleagues as "God's fellow workers" (1 Cor. 3:9). God has not called us to be tubes, but sons and daughters. Nor did he mean for us to be self-made men. As one wag put it, self-made men only demonstrate the horror of unskilled labor. God has called us to be co-workers.

Co-workers, but Not Co-equals

To say that we are co-workers with God is not to say that we are his co-equals. God is not, as popular wisdom would have it, anybody's co-pilot. From beginning to end, even our freedom is a gift from God. In Paul's letter to the Philippians, he urges them to "continue to work out your salvation with fear and trembling, for it is God who works in you to will and to act according to his good purpose" (2:12b, 13).

We are told to work out what God has worked in, to cooperate with what God has started and will sustain in us. Even what we give to God was first given to us by him.

Paderewski was, at one time, both the prime minister of Poland and a virtuoso pianist. A story is told about a mother who brought her young son to hear him perform. The boy

was just beginning to learn the piano and she wanted him
to hear a master, so she bought tickets for two front row seats
in the concert hall. They sat down a few minutes before the
concert was to begin.

In the excitement of the event, the mother was looking
around the large hall, mesmerized by the glitter and festiv-
ity. She didn't notice when her son climbed up on the stage,
walked over to the piano and sat down on the bench. Suddenly she, and everyone else in the auditorium, could hear
the tune "Chopsticks" coming from the piano on the stage.
To her embarrassment and horror, she turned to discover
that her son was committing this sacrilege upon the master's
piano.

Before she could get up on the stage and stop the boy,
the master himself walked out from behind the curtains.
Paderewski smiled at the distraught mother and waved her
back to her seat. He then stood behind the boy, reached
around him with both hands and began to play a lovely obli-
gato to his "Chopsticks." They were co-workers, but not
co-equals.

We become co-workers with God only when he reaches
around the feeble work of our hands with his hands and sanc-
tifies it. And our work is sanctified only when it is offered to
him as *sacramentum*.

Priests First, Then Kings

Think back for a moment to what God commanded the
first humans to do with the creation. He made them stewards
of his world. A steward is one who manages property for the
owner. A steward is a representative of the owner's authority.
God made us to be kings over the creation, serving under
him, the King. But we are kings only if we are first priests. A
priest is one who stands before God as a representative of
his people and offers sacrifices on their behalf. In regard
to our work in God's world, we offer all we do in the world

as a sacrifice of praise and devotion to God. Again, George
Herbert grasped this essential truth when he wrote,

> Man is the world's high-priest: he doth present
> The sacrifice for all . . . .[8]

Only to us has God made known his ways, says Herbert.
What the rest of the creation cannot do for itself, we must do
on its behalf: offer up to God as living sacrifices ourselves,
our work and the world. We do not learn to work well until
we first learn to worship well.

In Communion is the perfect embodiment of the mystery of human work. Communion shows dramatically the indissoluble link between the bread for which we all must toil
and slave, and the bread which God gives as a gift. We pray
for our daily bread, which God so richly provides as *sacramentum,* even though we must work for it. We offer it and
ourselves back to him as *sacramentum,* and it comes back to
us again as *sacramentum.* Christ nourishes our souls with the
very things we bring to him—things he first gave to us.

And so it goes, a blessed cycle of God's gift and our
offering of work and his gift and our sacrifice, on and on and
on. Everything we offer to God in faith and love comes back
to us, like the five loaves, blessed and sanctified. Communion
is God's oath to me that, because of Christ's love, all that I am
and all the work I do can be sanctified and made holy.

> Hope is hearing the melody of the future.
> Faith is to dance to it.
>
> *Rubem Alves*[1]

EPILOGUE: ∽

Something to Hope For

The words were cute, but they still stung when I read them. A two-year-old child had just learned how wonderful heaven was going to be, and was announcing that she, her Mommy and her younger sister Leah were going there. Her Daddy asked, "What about me?" She explained, "O no. You have to go to work!"[2]

The words stung because they touched a raw spot in my daily work. I fear there are times my own children would make the same observation: Daddy is too busy working to go to heaven. The necessities of life in the here and now crowd out the possibilities of life in the there and then. And all I do now seems so often to be going nowhere; at best my work seems like a mad scramble just to keep my nose above water. I wonder, does all the work I do make any difference, does it mean anything? Like the Teacher of Ecclesiastes, I am asking, "What does man gain from all his labor at which he toils under the sun?" (Eccl. 1:3)

140

Thomas Chalmers was right. The grand essentials of happiness are something to do, something to love and something to hope for. But the last essential may be the most essential, for without it the other two come up short. Do and love, work and worship, need hope to have meaning.

Work, this side of the Fall, can be, in fact often is, sheer toil and drudgery. I have a pastor acquaintance who serves an inner city church in the Eastern United States. As he heard me expound the New Testament teaching that all work, even the most menial, can be touched by God when done for God, he shook his head and said, "I know that's true, but I don't know how I can possibly explain it to half the members of my church." Half of his church members are either collecting unemployment, or when they are working, it is at the local car wash or standing dazed before an assembly line. Not only are they not making enough money to live, the work they are doing appears to be pointless.

But it's not just the poor who feel this way. My church, which is in a wealthy suburb in Orange County, is filled with people making very good salaries, but at a loss to understand how the work they do has any meaning beyond a paycheck. I hear them wondering, *What difference does it make that we help to create a better computer, or sell a good insurance policy?*

Worship struggles with the same questions. All it takes is one flat, dispirited worship service to get me wondering, *Does it really make any difference that we sing all those hymns, mutter all those prayers and listen to all those sermons? Does water, bread and wine really have any meaning? Is worship going anywhere?*

Without hope, something to do and something to love are simply not enough to make us happy. If worship in the here and now is "tuning our instruments,"[3] then there had better be a symphony some day. If work, in the here and now, even the most common, can be done as unto the Lord, then there had better be a time when we can hear him say, "Well done!"

"Well Done . . . Come In!"

That is precisely what Jesus promises to those who have done their work "as for" him (Col. 3:23). He will one day congratulate each of us and say, "Well done, good and faithful servant. . . . Come and share your master's happiness" (Matt. 25:21). The same kind of reward awaits those who have faithfully worshiped God now, tuning their instruments for the symphony to come. One of the pictures of heaven in the Book of Revelation is of God on his throne and his people worshiping him as "he who sits on the throne . . . spread(s) his tent over them" (7:15b). This is an allusion to the Exodus when God's presence with his people was symbolized by the Tent, or Tabernacle that housed the Holy of Holies. Then, only the priest could enter the Tent and enjoy that kind of intimacy with God. But in heaven, God spreads his tent, his presence, over all his people in intimate communion. That means in heaven we will be welcomed into the very heart of reality itself—the reality we can only strain to see in worship here on earth.

We've all had hints of what this means. In the summer of 1975, my wife Lauretta and I hiked the trail that runs along the crest of the Grand Tetons in Wyoming. On the first day of the hike we were walking north, toward the Grand Teton peak itself. We could look below in any direction and see 100 miles into Idaho and Wyoming. But what took our breath away was the Grand peak. It seemed to knife its way into the sky through the clouds that clung to its summit. Its beauty and power made me ache inside.

Why the sweet ache? C. S. Lewis said there are two reasons. One is the pain of separation: I was looking at something whose beauty drew me into it, but which I could not enter. In fact, the closer I got to the mountain, the more its loveliness seemed to elude me, withdraw and disappear. The other is the ache of loneliness. I was looking at something that so gripped my attention, but which was paying no attention to me. You might say I was "in love" with the mountain, but it didn't even know I existed.[4]

But suppose the mountain were to speak to me as I stood gazing at it, aching in longing and loneliness? Suppose it were to say, "Hello, Ben. I have known you from all eternity. I want you to be with me. Come closer to me, come into me and be as close to me as you can possibly be and still be yourself." Such is heaven's reward for those who have gazed faithfully at God here on earth. Such is the hope that animates the whole of Christian existence, our work and our worship. It is the reward of communion with the God for whom we did our work and to whom we offered our worship.

This Is All We Can Do . . . Now

Our hope is in more than congratulations and communion. It is in God's promise that everything we did for him, including our common work and our common worship, will not be in vain. It will all one day come to fulfillment and completion in the resurrection. At the end of the apostle Paul's paean to the resurrection, in 1 Corinthians 15, he concludes, "Therefore, my dear brothers, stand firm. Let nothing move you. Always give yourselves fully to the work of the Lord, because you know that your labor in the Lord is not in vain" (v. 58). In this particular context, the work Paul is speaking of is specifically Christian work, things like acts of charity and witness. But since he says in both his Ephesian and Colossian letters (Eph. 6:7; Col. 3:23) that only work can be done "as for" the Lord, we can include the things we do from nine to five, Monday through Friday, under the category of things we do that will not be in vain. If the Bible teaches anything about Christian living, it teaches that all of life is sacred and all we do is to be done as worship.

Nothing done for the Lord is accomplished in vain; sin and death have lost their final power over our work. I am acutely and gratefully aware of that as I write this the epilogue to my first book. I have worked long and hard on it. My family and friends will be proud of me when it is finally published. I will be proud of me. But there is one place I can go that, if I am not careful, will thoroughly depress me about what I am doing: a used book store. There, in dusty stacks, are the life-works, the *magnus opi,* of hundreds of men and women whose family and friends were every bit as impressed with them as mine will be with me—forgotten, for the most part, and selling for 35 cents apiece! In some ways it's good for me to walk into those stores and be reminded of the sobering truth that nothing I do has much significance in itself. But the promise of the resurrection is that, in Christ, my work will be raised with me; that somehow God will weave the frazzled threads of my life and work them into his great tapestry of salvation.[5]

That hope delivers us from the despair that nothing we do matters, and enables us to tackle even the most menial job with vigor. Elmer Bendiner tells the remarkable story of a B-17 bomber that flew a bombing mission over Germany in the latter days of World War Two. The plane was hit several times by shells and flak, with some of the hits directly in the fuel tank. Miraculously, the bomber did not explode. When it landed, eleven unexploded twenty-millimeter shells were taken out of the fuel tank! The shells were dismantled, and to the amazement of everyone, all were empty of explosives. Inside of one shell was a note written in Czech. Translated, it read, "This is all we can do for you now."[6] A member of the Czech underground, working in a German munitions factory, had omitted the explosives in at least eleven of the twenty-millimeter shells on his assembly line.

That worker must have wondered often if the quiet work he was doing to subvert the Nazi war effort was going to make any difference whatsoever to the outcome of the war. He may have died wondering. So it is with our work. We may not see now the place in God's plan our work as a secretary or waiter or telephone repairman occupies. But his promise that work done in the Lord is not in vain fortifies us against despair.

Lord . . . Teach Us to Dance!

That is the hope we celebrate in worship and which motivates us in our work. Rubem Alves defines hope as "hearing the melody of the future" and faith as dancing to it in the present.[7] Like joggers running with the headphones of their Sony "Walkmans" affixed to their ears, we Christians hear a melody no one else can hear. We hum along and tap our feet to it as we go about our work and worship. As we do, the promised future invades the present and our work and worship are filled with joy and energy.

In the brilliant film adaptation of Nikos Kazanzakis' *Zorba the Greek,* Zorba and his "Boss" sink all their assets into a wild scheme to haul lumber down from a mountain to the ocean. The logs will slide down cables right to a dock where they will be shipped to a lumber mill. The plan is that the saved labor costs in hauling the lumber down cables instead of on carts will make them millions of dollars. But the whole plan collapses when the cables break apart under the weight of the logs. In the final scene of the film, Zorba and the "Boss" stand looking at their monumental business failure. The sun is setting on the horizon. The two look at each other in silence. What is there left to say? It has all come to nothing. But the "Boss," a man tortured by his fear to let go of himself and live life as it comes, says to Zorba, "Zorba, teach me to dance!" The film ends with the two men dancing amid the wreckage of their work.

That is a picture of the effect our hope in Christ should have on our work, even the apparent wreckage of our work. Because we hear the melody of the future, we can dance amid wreckage, knowing that God will redeem even our failures. The disciples asked Jesus, "Lord, teach us to pray." Might that not also be another way of asking, "Lord, teach us to dance"?

Not Worth Comparing

A reward for our work and worship. A guarantee that they have meaning. Together they say this: whatever we are doing now, whatever we must struggle with now, are not worth comparing to the fulfillment of God's promise. The worst defeat this world can dish out will be swallowed up in victory; the best it can offer will pale and disappear in comparison with the world to come.

Blessed is the man or woman who gets even a glimpse of the future in the present. The medieval monk and philosopher Thomas Aquinas was one such person. His *Summa Theologica* is one of the greatest intellectual achievements of Western Civilization. A monumental work of thirty-eight treatises, three thousand articles and ten thousand objections, the *Summa* is one of the few attempts in all of Christian history to achieve a unified view of all truth—art, science, anthropology, psychology, ethics, philosophy, political theory, literature, everything—under God. Many would argue it is the only attempt that ever succeeded.

But Aquinas quit his work abruptly. On December 6, 1273, while celebrating Mass in the chapel of St. Nicholas, he had a profound mystical experience. After that, he announced to his secretary Reginald that he would write no more. Horrified, Reginald urged him to reconsider. Thomas tried to explain: "Reginald, I can do no more; such things have been revealed to me that all I have written seems to me as so much straw. Now, I await the end of my life after that of my works."[8] Firm in his resolve, he wrote no more until his death, about a year later.

Compared to the *Summa*, the work that you and I will do seems like nothing. But compared to what Thomas saw of the kingdom of heaven, the *Summa* seemed, as he put it, like "so much straw." At first, that sounds like a negation of human work. But it is not so much a negation of work as it is a celebration of the Christian hope. Even the best we do now is no more than a candle before the sun of God's goodness. A man with Thomas' towering intellect could say that. He accomplished exceedingly more than you and I could even dream, and yet he discovered that, when compared to the God who gave him his work to do, the work he did was pitifully small. God was the author of his work, and its end. So it is for all of us. By his mercy we work and worship now. By his mercy, our work and worship somehow matter to him. By his mercy our work will one day be over, at least as we know it now.

That is our grand hope. It is the essential of the essentials, the grandest of the grand. It is what makes the doing and the loving, the work and the worship so happy.

Maranatha! Come, Lord Jesus!

Notes

Chapter 1

1. Gordon Cosby, *Letters to Scattered Pilgrims*, quoted in *Parables, etc.* (Saratoga, CA: Saratoga Press) August 1983, 1.
2. Dorothy Sayers, "Why Work?" in *Creed or Chaos?* (New York: Harcourt, Brace and Co., 1949), 53.
3. Ibid., 54.
4. *Los Angeles Times*, 17 March 1985.

Chapter 2

1. Studs Terkel, *Working* (New York: Pantheon Books, 1972), xi.
2. Frederick Buechner, *Wishful Thinking* (New York: Harper and Row, 1973), 88.

Chapter 3

1. John Donne, *Donne, Poetical Works*, Herbert J. C. Grierson, ed. (London: Oxford University Press, 1979), 290 (emphasis mine).
2. From *Prayers for the Christian Year*, quoted in *A Guide to Prayer for Ministers and Other Servants*, Reuben P. Job and Norman Shawchuck, eds., *The Upper Room*, 267 (emphasis mine).
3. George Herbert, "The Elixir," in *The Complete Works in Verse and Prose of George Herbert* (Fuller Worthies' Library, 1874; New York: AMS Press, Inc.), 212.

Chapter 4

1. Karl Barth, *Church Dogmatics*, vol. 3, part IV, 615.

Chapter 5

1. A. W. Tozer, *The Pursuit of God* (Harrisburg, PA: Christian Publications, Inc., 1948), 127.
2. Quoted in *Context*, 15 November 1981, 6.
3. John Bisagno, *Positive Obedience* (Grand Rapids: Zondervan, 1979), quoted in *Pastor's Professional Research Service.*
4. Dr. S. D. Gordon, quoted in *Encyclopedia of 7700 Illustrations*, Paul Lee Tan, ed. (Rockville, MD: Assurance Publishers, 1979), number 659.
5. G. K. Chesterton, *Orthodoxy* (Garden City, NY: Doubleday and Co., Image Books, 1959), 159, 160.
6. George Herbert, "Man's Medley," in *The Complete Works in Verse and Prose of George Herbert* (Fuller Worthies' Library, 1874; New York: AMS Press, Inc.), 149.
7. "Our Life is Hid with Christ in God," Ibid., 58.
8. Hudson Taylor, quoted in *Encyclopedia of 7700 Illustrations*, number 3091.
9. I am told that Kuyper said this at his inaugural address for the Free University of Amsterdam.
10. William Barclay, *The Letters to the Galatians and Ephesians*, Daily Bible Study Series (Philadelphia: The Westminster Press, 1958), 215.
11. Quoted in *Leadership Journal* (Fall 1984): 46.
12. John Calvin, quoted in *Encyclopedia of 7700 Illustrations*, number 5095.
13. Herbert, "The Elixir," 212.

Chapter 6

1. C. S. Lewis, *Reflections on the Psalms* (New York: Harcourt, Brace Jovanovich, 1964), 97.
2. Ibid.

Chapter 7

1. I first encountered the idea of ritual drama in an engaging little book by John Wiley Nelson, *Your God Is Alive and Well in Popular Culture* (Philadelphia: The Westminster Press). His discussion of its meaning in connection with popular culture led me to begin thinking of it in relation to worship.

2. As fine a treatment as I have ever read of this marvelous scripture passage is found in Vernard Eller's *The Most Revealing Book of the Bible* (Grand Rapids: Eerdmans, 1974).
3. Sören Kierkegaard, *For Self Examination* (Minneapolis: Augsburg, 1940).
4. C. S. Lewis, *Mere Christianity* (New York: The Macmillan Co., 1960), 111.
5. ———, *Reflections on the Psalms* (New York: Harcourt, Brace, Jovanovich, 1964), 97.
6. Dorothy Sayers, "Why Work?" in *Creed or Chaos?* (New York: Harcourt, Brace, and Co., 1949), 59.
7. Ibid., 57.
8. Simone Weil, "Reflection on the Right Use of School Studies with a View to the Love of God," retold by Belden C. Lane in "Stalking a Snow Leopard: A Reflection on Work," *The Christian Century*, 4–11 January 1974, 15.
9. Martin Buber, quoted by Lane, Ibid.

Chapter 8

1. George Herbert, "The Elixir," in *The Complete Works in Verse and Prose of George Herbert* (Fuller Worthies' Library, 1874; New York: AMS Press, Inc.), 212.
2. Rabbi Abraham Heschel, anecdote quoted by Richard John Neuhaus in *Freedom for Ministry* (New York: Harper and Row, 1984).
3. Quoted by Martin Marty, *The Fire We Can Light* (New York: Doubleday and Co., 1973).
4. Herbert, "Evensong," 71.
5. Ibid.
6. Belden C. Lane, "Stalking the Snow Leopard: A Reflection on Work," *The Christian Century*, 4–11 January 1984, 13–15.
7. Frederick Buechner, *Wishful Thinking* (New York: Harper and Row, 1973), 95.

Chapter 9

1. Voltaire, quoted in *Encyclopedia of 7700 Illustrations*, Paul Lee Tan, ed. (Rockville, MD: Assurance Publishers, 1979), number 1387.
2. George Herbert, "Sunday," in *The Complete Works in Verse and Prose of George Herbert* (Fuller Worthies' Library, 1874; New York: AMS Press, Inc.), 84.
3. C. S. Lewis, *The Silver Chair* (New York: The Macmillan Co., 1953), 127.
4. Christopher Lasch, *The Culture of Narcissism* (New York: W. W. Norton, 1979), 7.
5. *Los Angeles Times.*

6. Rabbi Abraham Heschel, *The Sabbath* (New York: Farmer, Straus and Giroux, Inc., 1975), 8.
7. Ibid.
8. Ibid.
9. Henry Zylstra, *Testament of Vision* (Grand Rapids: Eerdmans, 1961).

Chapter 10

1. W. Jardine Grisbrooke, "Anaphora," in *The Westminster Dictionary of Worship*, J. G. Davis, ed. (Philadelphia: The Westminster Press, 1972), 15.
2. Annie Dillard, *Pilgrim at Tinker Creek* (New York: Harper's Magazine Press, 1974), 9.
3. Alan Richardson, *The Biblical Doctrine of Work* (London: SCM Press, 1952), 73.
4. Ibid., 69, 70.
5. Frederick Buechner, *Wishful Thinking* (New York: Harper and Row, 1973), 83.
6. George Herbert, "The Elixir," in *The Complete Works in Verse and Prose of George Herbert* (Fuller Worthies' Library, 1874; New York: AMS Press, Inc.), 212.
7. Peter Gillquist, *The Physical Side of Being Spiritual* (Grand Rapids: Zondervan, 1979), 143–150.
8. Herbert, "Providence," 132.

Epilogue

1. Rubem Alves, *Tomorrow's Child* (New York: Harper and Row, 1972), 195.
2. Quoted by Mary Alice Parks, *Focus on the Family Magazine*, October 1986, 7.
3. C. S. Lewis, *Reflections on the Psalms* (New York: Harcourt, Brace, Jovanovich, 1964), 97.
4. C. S. Lewis, *The Weight of Glory* (Grand Rapids: Eerdmans, 1977), 4, 5.
5. This lovely thought was suggested to me in the words of a prayer by Glenn Clark: "Let the threads of my life be interwoven with the tapestry of Your eternal purposes." Quoted from "Daily Prayer Companion," by Bob and Michael W. Benson, *Disciplines for the Inner Life* (Waco, TX: Word, Inc., 1985), 76.
6. Elmer Bendiner, *The Fall of Fortresses*, quoted in *Parables, etc.*, June 1983, 3.
7. Alves, 195.
8. Story told by Jacques Maritain, cited by R. C. Sproul in *Chosen Vessels*, Charles Turner, ed. (Ann Arbor: Vine Books, Servant Publications, 1985), 79.

Study Guide

1. Work—Blessing or Curse?

1. How would you answer the question, "Why do you work?"
2. How do you feel about the statement on p. 16, "Work is a gift and a blessing from God?"
3. Can you apply the stewardship role to your lifestyle?
4. Discuss the statement, "Our dignity comes from what we have done with what has been given to us" (p. 18).
5. Discuss the interview with Charles Schulz recorded on pp. 24–25, particularly the last sentence.

2. Take This Job and Shove It!

1. What is the Bible's answer to the question, "What went wrong with work?"
2. What is the first thing sin did to work?
3. Discuss the statement on p. 33: ". . . the tendency of work in a fallen world is to make the worker not the ruler but the slave of work . . . ."
4. Discuss the author's conclusion: "Worry, anxiety, insecurity—these are the things that lie behind greed and avarice" (p. 34).

3. Is There Any Hope?

1. Discuss the question, "How does Jesus save our work from the fatal infection of sin and death?"
2. Analyze the author's claim on p. 39: "When God, not the work, is our security, then the work we do can take on a certain joy and even wonder."
3. "Immensity cloistered in a womb—and in a room." Discuss these two elements in the life and ministry of Christ.
4. "Both the workbench and the Lord's Table can be approached in faith" (p. 43). What does this statement mean?
5. Can you (do you) do all your work as unto the Lord? If not, why not?

4. One Vocation, Many Occupations

1. What is the difference between "vocation" and "occupation," "Calling" and "callings"?
2. Discuss: ". . . each calling must become a theatre in which to pursue our "Calling.""
3. What happens when we consider the ultimate responsibility in our occupation to be unto God, not whoever or whatever is over us humanly speaking?
4. On p. 54 Patterson says, "A Christian has rights, but he or she always has duties before rights." What does this distinction mean?
5. Discuss the idea of living life as a "walk."

5. New Reasons for Work

1. As you consider your "calling" or occupation, why do you work?
2. On p. 59 Patterson says, "Union with Christ is also the root of all Christian ethics." Discuss the ramifications of this statement.
3. Discuss the word picture described by G. K. Chesterton on p. 59.
4. What does it mean to "do . . . all in the *name* of the Lord Jesus"?
5. Discuss the meaning of the heading on p. 63: "New Boss, New Diligence, New Holiness."
6. What is the "salary" for this kind of work?

6. Worship Is Forever

1. What is the first reason worship is important?
2. What is the second? The third?
3. On p. 83 the author says, "Work ceases to be worship if it is not cultivated in specific, symbolic acts of works, regularly and often." Discuss.
4. "In worship we tune our spirits for the praise of God. We also tune our ears to hear him in the world" (p. 84). Discuss.

7. The Great Drama

1. How does the author define "ritual drama"?
2. Who is the performer and who is the audience in the ritual drama in heaven?
3. What happens to worship when we see God at the center rather than ourselves?
4. How do you react to the author's description of the role of the sermon in worship?
5. Discuss the Dorothy Sayers' quote on p. 95: "The only Christian work is good work well done."
6. What do you feel is the purpose of work?

8. A Story within a Story

1. "If secularism says nothing means anything, Christianity says everything means everything" (p. 94). Discuss.

2. What does it mean "to 'play' the Drama of our salvation . . . in worship" (p. 101)?
3. What does the liturgy of the sanctuary tell us about the liturgy of the world?
4. The author says, "There ought to be a kind of playfulness about our work" (p. 104). What does he mean?
5. "God can be seen and encountered in drudgery and the tedious" (p. 105). Discuss.
6. Discuss Buechner's comment, "The place God calls you is the place where your deep gladness and the world's deep hunger meet."
7. Discuss the two exhibits of life's essence with which Patterson concludes the chapter. How would you like to be remembered by your family and friends?

9. *Never on Sunday*

1. What "Sunday" rules do you remember from your childhood?
2. In what two ways do we "violate" the Sabbath?
3. What does the word "Sabbath" mean?
4. Discuss the Scripture, "For we are God's workmanship, created in Christ Jesus to do good works . . . ." What effect should this have on our attitude toward work?
5. Examine the Sabbath as a "freedom" day. Look at it as a day of "hope."
6. Discuss the Sabbath as a "window into the future" and a telescope of time.

10. *Our Daily Bread*

1. Discuss Communion as "celebration." How do you experience it?
2. "Communion is a mystery to wonder at, not an idea to argue over" (p. 128). React to this statement.
3. How should "offering" fit into "Communion"?
4. What is the "synergistic" view of work?
5. As Christians, we are to be stewards, priests and kings. Discuss.

Epilogue. Something to Hope For

1. "Do and love, work and worship, need hope to have meaning" (p. 141). What does Patterson mean by this?
2. How do you react to the author's "mountain" illustration on pp. 142–143?
3. Discuss Ruben Alves's definition of hope as "hearing the melody of the future" and faith as dancing to it in the present.